How to . . .

MW01482973

Buy A Great House!

The Step-by-Step Guide to Finding and Buying a Quality House

Kelly VanBuskirk, B.A., LL.B., LL.M.

DREAMCATCHER PUBLISHING
Saint John • New Brunswick • Canada

DreamCatcher Publishing acknowledges the support of the New Brunswick Arts Council.

Canadian Cataloguing in Publication Data

VanBuskirk, Kelly - 1967

Buy a Great House

ISBN - 1-894372-45-X

     1. House buying. I. Title.

HD1379.V36 2004   643'.12   C2004-904036-7

Editor: Yvonne Wilson

Typesetter: Chas Goguen

Cover Design: Dawn Drew, INK Graphic Design Services Corp.

Printed and bound in Canada

DREAMCATCHER PUBLISHING INC.
105 Prince William Street
Saint John, New Brunswick, Canada E2L 2B2
www.dreamcatcherbooks.ca

To Cynthia & Cecil, who make my house a GREAT home,

To my parents, who gave me a GREAT home in which to grow up; and

To my co-workers at Lawson & Creamer - which is a GREAT home away from home.

BUY A GREAT HOUSE

INDEX

INTRODUCTION

More than one once-happy home buyer has ended up miserable when a house turned out to be a lemon. Leaky basements, unusable wells, backed up sewage systems, faulty electrical systems, unexpectedly high heating bills - these are all common occurrences in the world of house transactions. Sadly, most of these problems are not easily (or cheaply) fixed. When a purchaser takes possession of a newly-bought home, therefore, the risk is that one or more serious flaw(s) will surface, costing the homeowner loads of time and money. On top of the repair expenses, house defects can totally disrupt your life, and lead to months of stress, anxiety and back-breaking labour. Even dumping the heartache can become difficult, since a house suffering from obvious defects is difficult to sell - even for an unscrupulous vendor who tries to hide the problems!

The surprising fact is that too many home purchasers still don't take proper precautions before purchasing. In the hustle and bustle of house hunting, buyers lull themselves into believing that someone else (such as the real estate agent, the lawyer or even the vendor) is making sure that only a great house will be purchased. *Nothing could be further from the truth!*

Remember this about house purchasing: while you can rely on other people for *some assistance*, **you** are the only person who knows what you like and what you don't like in a house, and what conditions are acceptable or unacceptable to you. No one else will *tell you* that you absolutely must (or must not) buy a particular property. The choice is ultimately yours. Additionally, there is a temptation to transfer responsibility for your decision-making to someone else: your real estate agent, for example, "is making money on the deal", and he or she should *make sure* that the house you buy is in excellent condition. . . right? **Wrong!** If the house has a defect that you can't see, what makes you think that your real estate agent *would* see it? Why would you believe that your lawyer (who probably hasn't even been in the house) would be able to protect you from the impact of that defect? The truth is that **you** are responsible for performing inspections, coordinating expert investigations and making the inquiries that you need in order to purchase a great house. **This book is designed to help!**

As you go about buying your next home, think about the amount of money you will spend. Before you agree to purchase any property, take all of the necessary precautions to protect your money and your peace of mind. While the following pages won't guarantee a trouble-free home purchase, they do provide you with concrete suggestions and ideas for avoiding future headaches (and heartaches). Make sure that *you* **Buy A Great House**.

WHERE TO FIND A GREAT HOUSE

Home buyers normally fall into one of three categories when it comes to the geographical area, or location, in which they want to live. First, there are some home-buyers who have already decided on a neighbourhood; for whatever reason, this type of purchaser wants to live in only one area, and no other location will do. Second, there are home-buyers who have just moved to their city or town and have no idea what neighbourhoods may be appropriate; and third, many home-buyers have a sense that *some* neighbourhoods may be appropriate for their needs, but are not familiar with all of the neighbourhoods they should consider.

If you are searching for a house to purchase, the location of that house will prove critically important to you from a number of perspectives. For example, the location will impact heavily on both the price of the home and its *value*; it will also be relevant in terms of where your children will go to school and participate in extra-curricular activities, and how long it will take you to travel to and from work. In short, the location of your home will affect virtually every aspect of your life. In order to make a wise decision on the location of your new house, you should seriously consider the following issues.

Factors in Choosing a Location

Location, location, location. The importance of a property's location has always been well-known. As a home-buyer, you should recognize that the current and future *value* of your property will be dictated by its location. A great house in a bad neighbourhood will never achieve its optimal value, for example, while an average house in a great neighbourhood will probably fetch prices in excess of its worth. Although most people do not buy a house with the intention of selling it immediately, you should always keep in mind that your circumstances could change on a moment's notice, and the sale of your house may become *necessary*. For that reason alone, you should consider buying a house in a neighbourhood you can afford.

Buying for Market Value

You may decide that the market value of a house is not important to you. If you are *absolutely certain* that you will not be moving from the house in the future, for example, then its future resale value may well be an insignificant consideration. For that matter, you may be so fabulously wealthy that the money aspect of your home is irrelevant. My bet, because you are reading this book, is that you are not in a position where the financial consequences of your decision make no difference. Assuming that is the case, here are some basic thoughts on finding a house with great market value.

A Great Neighbourhood

As stated above, since the mathematics will tell you that purchasing a great house in a great neighbourhood will leave you with a more saleable product than if you buy a great house in an average neighbourhood, think of it this way: Most people would be happier to live in a great neighbourhood. Regardless of a person's income level, their family status and even their age, great neighbourhoods are appealing because they offer a nice (and presumably safe) environment with some level of prestige or social acceptability. On the other hand, more average neighbourhoods will be acceptable (as they should be) to many people but not appealing to some upwardly mobile buyers. I am not suggesting that this is a fair (or even reasonable) truth; but only that it is *the truth*, and that this truth means that a great neighbourhood will produce a larger pool of potential buyers than an average neighbourhood.

The next limitation on any prospective buyers' pool is *price*. Obviously some buyers will like a particular neighbourhood but be unable to find a house in that neighbourhood which falls within their affordability range. Consequently even though a particular buyer may *want* to buy your house, he or she may be financially unable to do so. If your house is the best house in a great neighbourhood, then the price is likely high. As a consequence, the pool of potential buyers for your house will be relatively small. Though your house is the best house in an average neighbourhood, the pool of potential buyers will be small, since only *some buyers* will find your average neighbourhood acceptable. Within that already reduced pool of potential buyers, a further reduction will be made based on the price of your house, which is likely to be higher than some of the potential buyers in the pool can afford.

The moral of the story is that, in order to maximize the pool of potential buyers for your home in the future, you should consider purchasing a house in a great neighbourhood - but not the *greatest* house in that neighbourhood!

Points to Consider

Every neighbourhood has its features and its drawbacks. What may represent a feature to some home-buyers can, at the same time, be a drawback to other home buyers. Before you start actively searching for a house to buy, you should probably make a list of neighbourhood amenities that will be important to you - both now and in the future. Some of the usual points to consider are listed below.

Safety - almost every home-buyer will have some concern for neighbourhood safety. While your future safety, and

the safety of your family, cannot be guaranteed *in any neighbourhood*, some areas are obviously better than others. If a neighbourhood has a history of a high crime rate, for example, safety
will be an obvious concern. Similarly, if the area contains busy
streets, railway tracks or similar dangers, those should also be
considered. Finally, natural sources of danger (such as rivers,
lakes and cliffs) can be very beautiful and can increase nearby
property values; at the same time, though, they can be hazard-
ous, especially to young children. In assessing the safety of a
particular neighbourhood, you may want to consider these questions:

- Does the local police force maintain statistics on neighbourhood crime? In some areas the police record crime
  levels, and that information may disclose a pattern of
  crime in different sections of your city or town. Refer-
  ence to those statistics can be helpful in developing a
  sense of what goes on in each neighbourhood;

- How far away is the nearest police station? How far
  away is the nearest fire department and the nearest fire
  hydrant?
  Quite often, your homeowners insurance policy pre-
  mium will be affected by the answer to this last question. If there is a fire department and/or fire hydrant near
  your home, for example, homeowners insurance premi-
  ums may be reduced somewhat;

- Do the streets in the area have high traffic volume?
  Depending on your own circumstances, traffic issues
  may or may not worry you. If you have (or expect to
  have) young children, traffic has to be considered from
  a safety perspective. Even if you do not have young children, you should think about traffic volumes in the con-

text of when you would normally be using your street. You may find that bumper-to-bumper traffic is normal at the very time that you would leave for, and return from, work. If you know that situation would frustrate you on a daily basis, think twice about buying the house;

- Is the land unsafe? Is there a lake, river, cliff or forest nearby? If so, are you confident that you can manage the risk posed by it?
  Aside from natural dangers, are there any environmental concerns in the area? In this day and age, it is not uncommon for particular neighbourhoods to have environmental concerns arising from current or former industrial uses. You should look into the history of the area to make sure that there are no obvious sources of panic; remember, though, that people who live in the neighbourhood (particularly the person trying to sell you a house) may easily take an optimistic view of environmental issues since no one wants to admit that their property has been de-valued;

- How isolated is the house?
  Some people love their privacy; others only love the idea of privacy. Unless you have actually lived in an isolated area, you won't know for sure if you will truly love privacy, or if you only *think* you will. Personally, I like the idea of having neighbours within screaming distance. If you are the same way, don't buy an isolated house;

- Are there street lights in the neighbourhood? Keep in mind, if you buy a house in a neighbourhood without street lights, and if your nearest neighbours are not very near, it will be very dark at night;

- Are the roads relatively flat and in good condition?

Having grown up at the top of a very long, steep hill, I can confirm that steep streets can be dangerous. During the Winter months, snow and ice can make driving on any road (particularly a steep one) very treacherous. Furthermore, kids on bikes, skateboards, toboggans, scooters and every other type of vehicle have to be extremely careful in hilly neighbourhoods.

The *condition* of the roads in the neighbourhood deserves some consideration as well. Unfortunately conditions of the road may change and therefore should not be a fundamental consideration for you. At the back of your mind, however, remember that roads in poor condition can damage vehicles and, more importantly, can cause drivers to swerve and stop unpredictably - all of which can lead to accidents.

Facilities

Again, your current and future needs will dictate what facilities will be important features for your neighbourhood. Some of the top considerations are:

- *Schools* - if you have a need for schools, you will want to investigate the availability with care. Having a school nearby (especially for *young* children) is, naturally, attractive. Regardless of where the nearest school is located, you should ask: Do the children in the neighbourhood walk to school or take a bus? If they walk, are there safety concerns? How does the school rank for teaching and student success? What level of parent involvement does the school enjoy? What facilities does the school offer?

Unless you have the option of sending your child to a

private school, remember that your choice of a house will probably dictate what public school your child must attend. If the school is a dud, you will have to live with that reality for as long as you own the house. Your best bet is to thoroughly investigate schooling issues before you purchase, making sure that you talk to teachers and neighbourhood parents, and that you review statistics concerning the school which may be made available through your local government.

- *Hospitals* - the quality of nearby hospitals will likely not influence your decision on where to live - at least not in a substantial way. Nevertheless, it is worthwhile to familiarize yourself with the services available at the local hospital(s), so that you will understand what medical services can be obtained locally. *On a related note, you may want to find out if family physicians are readily available in the area and, if not, whether there are acceptable medical clinics.*

- *Recreation* - some communities have a lot more recreational facilities to offer than others. If you have children, you likely know that the availability of these facilities can be very important, since many parents become painfully familiar with various ballfields, rinks and community centres. What *is* available in the neighbourhood? Will the local facilities meet your recreational needs and the needs of your family members? Are there any movie theatres, fitness centres or other attractions nearby?

- *Shopping* - some neighbourhoods are quite a distance from the nearest store. You may be able to cope with that (and even enjoy it) as long as you are a careful planner. I suspect, however, that an absence of stores can be deeply frustrating when you run out of milk just before supper, have a child with a high fever and you are out of medicine, or you break your shoelaces on the way to an important meeting.

The reality of modern life is that most of us *need* to have access to stores. You should honestly consider the extent of your needs and assess each neighbourhood accordingly. Chances are that most neighbourhoods will offer at least a basic store for last-minute purchases; you may have to eliminate some potential neighbourhoods, though, if the distance to a real grocery store (for example) is prohibitive.

- *Churches* - the availability of churches may not be important to you. If it is important, you should assess it accordingly.

- *Distance to Work* - you should assess every potential neighbourhood in the context of its distance from your workplace. Your concern should be two-fold - what will be the travel cost involved? What will be the time required? Many people enjoy a lengthy drive to and from work each day. Their time spent in a car or bus amounts to relaxation and allows them to catch up on daily news or entertainment. Depending on your schedule, however, too much travel time can be a major frustration, and the cost of travel can also be a negative issue.

If everyone in your household is not a licenced driver with his or her own vehicle, it may be worthwhile to consider the availability of public transportation as well. Is the property near a bus route, for example? If not, you should decide if your own personal means of transportation will be sufficient. Think these matters over *be-*

fore you buy a house.

Conclusion

The location of your house can be as important as the house itself. If, on a whim, you buy a home which is poorly situated, you will likely regret that decision for as long as you live on the property. Remember that issues which seem like minor inconveniences during the excitement and exasperation of house-hunting can easily prove to be time, money and peace of mind-draining qualities in the course of every day life. Before you choose a neighbourhood, do your homework; make sure it meets your needs. Choose wisely!

RECRUITING A GREAT PURCHASE TEAM

We live in a complicated society. The demands which exist for an endless supply of products and services have made it so that very few people (if any) can be self-sufficient anymore. Unlike the cavemen, therefore, who apparently found and furnished their own caves, hunted their own meat and collected their own vegetables, our society is built on *specialization*. As tempting as it sometimes may be to do it yourself, there are many functions which should be left to experts, and house buying is no exception.

Buying property is not like buying most retail products. When you go into a department store to buy a sweater, for example, you already have some experience with sweaters, since you probably already have worn a few in your lifetime. Consequently, you know that any sweater you buy will wear out at some point, and that it can be ruined with one unfortunate accident. Fortunately, you also know that the price of most sweaters is not so high that your personal finances will be ruined if the sweater is. Quite often the same cannot be said about houses.

First, it is important to remember that houses are built with elements of science and engineering expertise. Even when an amateur builds his own house, the amateur puts designs and products to use which have been developed by experts. In fact, laws typically require the construction of houses to be done within certain levels of precision and, in some cases, qualified professionals *must* complete aspects of the work. For example, the installation of electrical wiring, plumbing and some mechanical components of houses must be completed by licensed experts. Consequently, no amateur handyman should feel completely at ease with the construction or inspection of a house. For that reason, a team of experts is very useful (if not essential) to finding (and ultimately buying) a great house.

The members of *your* team will depend somewhat on the type of house you are considering. Normally, home buyers engage the services of a real estate agent, a banker, a lawyer, a surveyor and a home inspector in the house purchasing process; in some cases, though, you may need additional team members - such as an electrician, a plumber, a stone mason, a furnace contractor and others. Knowing actually whom to include on your team - and why - is the first step to purchasing a great house.

Your Real Estate Agent

A real estate agent can be helpful in locating a potentially good house to purchase. Real estate agents have access to large numbers of houses which have been listed for sale with them and other real estate agents. Consequently, a good real estate agent will likely be aware of many more potentially acceptable houses than you could find yourself. In addition, qualified real estate agents have knowledge and expertise relating to market values and therefore can help you negotiate a purchase.

The problem with real estate agents is that some home buyers blindly trust their agent, with the naive expectation that the agent will point out every potential problem with a house as well as every possible difficulty in making a purchase agreement. *Remember this:*

Your real estate agent is probably not a qualified home inspector, nor does he or she likely know much more about a particular house than you do. Real estate agents' expertise lies in helping people buy and sell homes; they are not capable of noticing every house defect!

I sometimes have the feeling that home buyers expect their real estate agent to whip a crystal ball out of his or her pocket in order to predict the future of a particular property. Naturally, it would be terrific if real estate agents had that ability. Then your agent could *tell you* if the house you wanted to buy would leak, burn down because of faulty wiring, or cause you some other type of grief in the future. The problem, of course, is that no real estate agent has a crystal ball from which to read the future of a house. In fact, very few real estate agents have expertise in home inspection - a point made clear by many standard form agreements of purchase and sale. Quite often an agreement of purchase and sale will expressly stipulate that the purchaser requires an inspection of the property by a qualified home inspector. Now if the purchaser's real estate agent were an expert home inspector, it would be unnecessary to conduct another inspection, wouldn't it?

The benefit of having a real estate agent involved in your search for a new home lies in the agent's knowledge of the *local market*. Typically, a real estate agent will have access to a large listing of houses currently for sale, including homes which may have just been placed on the market. As a result, a good agent will be able to notify you of available homes which meet your requirements, and will direct you to potential purchase options in a time and cost-effective way.

Another benefit offered by most real estate agents is their knowledge of their local lay of the land. In other words, a good agent will be able to provide you with ideas on the characteristics of particular neighbourhoods which will help make your decision-making processes easier. If you have children, for example (or if you anticipate having children in the foreseeable future), a real estate agent should be able to direct you to the most popular neighbourhoods in your community for young families. Similarly, you may be at a point in life where you want to avoid family neighbourhoods, and your agent will likely have up to date information on the most popular locations which will suit your preferences.

Many home buyers and sellers try to avoid real estate agents with the hope that doing so will save them money. While it is true that agents charge commission fees on successful transactions (which are normally paid by the vendor of the house), the services of a good agent will almost always be worth the cost. If you are the seller, the real estate agent's fees will typically include extensive advertising costs, assistance with the agreement of purchase and sale, advice as to the most appropriate sale price and negotiating techniques and, most importantly, relief from the hassle and discomfort of showing your home to strangers. The purchaser should benefit from a real estate agent's involvement by having access to the agent's wealth of information regarding homes for sale on the market, as well as advice regarding typical market values in any given neighbourhood, convenience in having assistance with co-ordinating viewings of potential homes to purchase, assistance in the negotiation of an agreement of purchase and sale and, significantly, help with the co-ordination of home inspections, water tests, banking documents and transaction closing. Although it is certainly possible to buy a great house *without* the help of an experienced real estate agent, the agent does provide a valuable service, and you should not overlook the potential importance of that service just to save a few dollars. In fact, you may even end up overpaying for your house if you buy it without the guidance of an agent. The key, as with hiring any expert, is to find a real estate agent who will provide you with excellent service.

Your Banker

Unless you have independent wealth or the support of someone with independent wealth, bank funding will likely be necessary for any house purchase you intend to make.

Choosing the bank (and the banker) with whom you will do business is likely to depend on a number of factors. Here are some of them:

- Do you have (or could you have) a long-standing relationship with a particular banker? Although it may be tempting to make your choice of a bank based *solely* on the interest rate being offered, you should look at the larger picture. In this day and age, a person's banker can be an important friend (or foe). If you were to need a loan in the future, for example, wouldn't it be great to have a strong relationship with a banker who wanted to help you with your financial requirements? Additionally, don't you want to do business with a banker who will *tell you* about less than obvious financing options and who will alert you to any perks or advantages available? Before you sign up for the lowest mortgage interest rate, think about your future needs - and who can help you with them.

- Is the bank a stable, full-service institution with a great reputation? Every individual banker will be limited by the quality of his or her bank. For that reason, you should give some thought to the long-term stability of the bank in question. Does the bank always offer competitive benefits to its customers? While you don't necessarily need to (or want to) place your business with the front-runner in the banking industry, you should think twice about marginal players in the industry and companies which have not historically been in the lending industry.

- Naturally, the deal being offered by each bank is an important consideration. You will want to focus on the cheapest interest rate, and carefully examine the *true value* of perks offered. Sometimes, banks will offer cash back arrangements, free legal services and other benefits in exchange for your agreement to particular mortgage terms. The question you should answer before accepting these terms is whether or not the perks are actually worth the amount of the interest charges.

Overall, your banker will be a necessary part of your team, both in respect of this house purchase and of your future life. Don't be mesmerized by one banking consideration to the exclusion of others.

Your Home Inspector

Like most of the members of your house purchase team, a home inspector can make the difference between your future happiness or future misery. A *good* home inspector will steer you away from problem houses - not by telling you whether to buy or not buy, but by informing you of the types of repairs a particular building may need, either now or in the future. The key, then, is to hire a skilled and experienced inspector and thereafter to listen carefully to that person's advice!

Some buyers make the tragic mistake of believing that every home inspector is the same. You have to remember that in most places the home inspection occupation is not well-regulated. Unlike doctors, lawyers, accountants, plumbers and other specialists, many home inspectors have no specific qualification. For that reason, it is particularly important that you investigate potential home inspectors carefully. You should *at least* find a candidate who can confirm his or her training, experience and references. You may want to hire a civil engineer to perform your inspection. Regardless of the choice you make, be sure that your inspector has a wealth of experience, and check those references!

Another important point to be aware of is the *terms* of the inspector's arrangement with you. Some home inspectors require your signature on a very onerous standard form services agreement. The agreement may indicate, for example, that you *will not* make any claim against the home inspector for an amount in excess of his or her fees. Think about that for a moment. You hire a home inspector with the assumption that you will be warned about any significant problems with a house. On the day of the inspection, the inspector presents you with some paperwork that he needs you to sign. The inspector tells you that the paperwork is just an agreement that lets him do the inspection and confirms that you will pay him $300.00 for his report. Now the inspector isn't trying to mislead you; instead, he has a standard form contract, which he has been using for several years because the company that he works for (or his own lawyer) has recommended it. Because you have better things to do, and because the inspector is anxious to get started on his review of the property, neither of you reads through the agreement. Instead, both of you sign the document and go about your business. All of this will be fine *unless* you buy the house with the understanding that it is in good condition, only to learn later that your inspector missed a major foundation crack or some other defect. If it weren't for the agreement, you would likely be able to sue your inspector with ease to recover the damages you suffer because of his error. The existence of the agreement, however (particularly the limitation on the inspector's liability), makes your case much (much!) more difficult. Before you hire an inspector, therefore, make sure that you understand the terms of the agreement. Be very reluctant to sign any contract that attempts to limit the inspector's responsibility for mistakes in his report. Remember that an inspector should be willing to stand behind his or her work, and any attempt by the inspector to limit responsibility should make you suspicious. Furthermore, don't allow an inspector's insurance coverage to give you a false sense of security; just because an inspector has insurance does not mean that *you* will be able to access that insurance - especially if you've signed an agreement which effectively prevents you from suing!

The Inspector's Work - you should be present at the property during the inspection process. Most inspectors will state (quite fairly) that they cannot be held responsible for house defects which are hidden by walls or other obstacles. The question, though, is this: when is a defect actually hidden? In some cases, a foundation crack or other major problem may be simply difficult to see because of boxes or other storage items. Unless you know what the conditions were during the inspection, it will be difficult for you to argue, later, that the inspector ought to have identified a particular problem. If you are present during the inspection, you will be able to compare your observation with the inspector's written report while the *facts* are still fresh in your mind. Make sure you take the time to review your inspector's observations with him or her either during or at the conclusion of the session; if you wait until you receive the written inspection report, it may be difficult for the inspector to fully explain any concerns.

If your inspector does express concerns regarding any aspect of the property, be sure that you address them immediately and thoroughly. In most home purchases, it is the sole responsibility of the buyer to express concerns, to raise any deficiencies, and most agreements of purchase and sale allow only a very limited time to do so. In other words, if your inspector has pointed out a problem which concerns you, you may want to have the vendor share in the cost of any necessary repairs or, in severe situations, you may decide to abandon your purchase altogether. Unless you deal with those concerns immediately, you may be stuck with buying the house and repairing it yourself.

Your home inspector will be a critical player on your house purchase team. Choose wisely, and play an active role in the inspection itself. The more information you can gather about the condition of a house, the better decisions you will be able to make.

Your Lawyer

Trust me: lawyers are not the most popular people in our society. While lawyer jokes are always plentiful, what's *really funny* is that, when people have disputes, their lawyers are very quickly consulted. Obviously, some disputes cannot be resolved, except through the court process. The good news is that lawyers are not only capable of arguing over problems, we are also able to help people *avoid* problems.

The average home buyer (and seller) probably thinks of his lawyer as a necessary evil in the home buying process. That may because you pay the lawyer for *work*, rather than for something concrete (such as a couch, a chair or even a paint job). In fact, unlike the work of a dentist, your lawyer's work is not even done in your presence, for the most part. Not only are you unsure what it's about, you don't even get the chance to see it happening!

Just because you can't see everything that your lawyer is doing, don't assume the work has no value. Quite to the contrary, your lawyer helps to ensure that you have good title to the land that you are buying, that your mortgage arrangements are made with your bank, that the documents needed by your bank are prepared and signed, that the vendor's lawyer provides a proper deed to the land (and this is critical, since an incorrect deed could result in your *never actually owning the property!*). Additionally, your lawyer can help to ensure that the obligations of both sides, (which are outlined in the agreement of purchase and sale) are met. Finally, your lawyer co-ordinates the funds needed to purchase the land (obviously, a fundamental aspect of any transaction), and he makes sure that your deed and mortgage are properly registered in the land registry system. On that note, failure to register your legal documents can have a grave impact on your claim to ownership of the property.

My recommendation is that you find a lawyer you like, one whom you can work with easily. Make sure any lawyer you choose has experience, and don't overlook recommendations from friends and relatives. If someone you trust has had a good experience with a particular lawyer, that's a good sign.

Before you choose a lawyer, find out what *all* of the costs will be. Remember that a lawyer's *fees* are only part of the equation; you will also be charged government registration fees, photocopying costs and other expenses. You will save yourself a shock if you investigate these costs in advance.

In addition to knowing the cost of the lawyer's services, you should develop some understanding of how that person works. Most lawyers are very busy and, therefore, they typically have staff members who contact you with information or questions concerning your transaction. Before you choose a lawyer, though, make sure that either the lawyer or a staff member will be reasonably available to answer any questions you may have, or to deal with any concerns which may arise. Nothing will frustrate you more if, while you are attempting to purchase your house, you are unable to obtain information from your lawyer.

In the end, your lawyer will play an important role in concluding your house transaction while, at the same time, protecting your interests. Be sure to facilitate a good relationship with your lawyer but, at the same time, promptly express any concerns you have about his or her service. Since you are the person who stands to gain (or lose) in the transaction, you need to be satisfied with the way it is handled.

Your Land Surveyor

You may be tempted to accept an old land survey certificate from the vendor of a house. While an old survey certificate can provide helpful information to you, it should not be accepted as a replacement for an up-to-date survey. Believe it or not, important issues concerning land boundaries can change over time, and the cost of a current survey plan is small in relation to the risk you will incur in not having one. For example, it is possible that a surveyor who has made a mistake in an old survey certificate can successfully argue that you have no grounds to sue the surveyor for his mistake since, technically, the mistake was made for someone else and not you. You can imagine how frustrated you will be if you base your decision to buy your property on a surveyor's report which was prepared for the vendor and, sometime later, you learn that the report is inaccurate. When you try to have the surveyor correct the problem (or answer for his or her mistake if the problem is beyond fixing) you will not appreciate the complications which arise in favour of the surveyor (and against you).

All of the same rules which apply to choosing the other members of your team should also apply to your selection of a surveyor. While the surveyor typically plays one of the final roles in your home purchase exercise, it is not an insignificant responsibility, and you should not take it lightly.

Overall, the members of your house purchase team are very important players. Each one of them supplies special skills which can save you a lifetime of dissatisfaction and, also, a truckful of money. Don't underestimate the value of your team;

select experts who have proven track records and with whom you are comfortable. Once you've put your team of experts together, listen to their advice! You *need* their help.

HOW TO DO A GREAT HOME INSPECTION

The truth is that some people spend more time and effort buying much smaller items - like cars and even toasters - than they put into buying their *home*! It makes absolutely no sense that the same person who researches vehicle models in consumer reports, takes test drives, examines each car with great care for even the most minor of flaws, has it examined by a mechanic and demands a warranty from the car dealer would spend 4 or 5 times as much money (or more) on a house, without nearly as much diligence. *Why would you be so careless?*

The Money Pit

Back in the 1990s, Tom Hanks starred in a movie called The Money Pit, which is a film about a young married couple who buy the house of their dreams. The dream turns into a nightmare, when every conceivable problem with the house arises. Pipes burst, floors collapse ... basically, the building disintegrates before their very eyes! The two central characters pour more and more money into renovations and repairs - all the while becoming completely disgusted. The home that was supposed to bring happiness to the couple nearly ruins their lives. *And that could be you.*

If you don't remember anything else from the pages of this book, *remember this*: **you cannot be too careful in the process of buying a house!**

I have never seen a money-back guarantee given to the purchaser of a home. If the house you buy ends up being a lemon, you're stuck with it; you can't take it back for a full refund and you can't exchange it for another one. Even when you ask for written warranties concerning the house from the former owner, you have to keep in mind that those warranties are typically not as helpful as you may think. In many cases, you would have to sue the former owner to get any compensation at all; in turn the lawsuit process would likely require you to *prove* the exact cause of your problems *and* the former owner's knowledge of those problems. The steps in that process are, of course, time consuming, frustrating and costly - with no assurance of success. If you do ultimately win in court against the former owner, collecting your compensation can be another gruelling (and possibly unsuccessful) procedure. If the former owner has no assets, for example, you may not be able to recover any money at all. As the old saying goes: you can't squeeze blood from a stone!

What all of this means is that you have to take all possible precautions *before* you buy your house. Take the time *now*, before you even start looking at houses (and certainly before you make a purchase offer) to develop a self-protection plan.

Think It Over

Think about this: every house has a number of components which involve special expertise. The structural components (including the foundation, the walls and the roof) require structural design expertise; the water pipes demand the expertise of a plumber; an electrician has to install the wiring and fixtures; the heating and air exchange systems require special knowledge, and the list goes on. Now, ask yourself how much of that expertise you have *yourself*? Be honest - don't give yourself more credit than you deserve! For most of us, the answer has to be none. Some people have limited expertise in one or two fields, but very, very few people have expertise in all (or even most) of the components of a house. Consequently, it is equally true that very, very few people are qualified to properly inspect an entire home. If you want to know all of the strengths and weaknesses of any property, therefore, you will have to call on a variety of experts to assist you. Here are some thoughts on issues which will require expert inspection and diagnosis.

Land Inspection

Before you even look at the exterior and interior of any house, you should educate yourself on the condition of the *surrounding land*. I'm not talking about the *value* of the land, either. Questions concerning land values can be best answered by real estate appraisers and real estate agents, and are addressed in an earlier chapter. The *condition* of the land you are thinking of purchasing is important because it may require costly maintenance and improvements in the future. Some of the issues to be examined are:

Entry

Does the property have a driveway? If so, you should think about the following questions:

- Is the driveway flat or steep? If it's steep, does it present potential water drainage problems or difficulty using it (particularly during the Winter months)?

- Is the driveway made of gravel, concrete or pavement? Does it require any repair? Even if it does not *now* require repairs, could it have to be fixed in the future? Keep in mind that most driveways will require maintenance and repairs at some point, and you should determine how often work will be required and how much it will cost.

- Is the driveway long or short? If you live in a cold climate, how will you deal with snow removal? While a long driveway can provide privacy, it can also be a severe burden in snowy weather.

Lawns and Gardens

A beautiful lawn and garden can be a great asset for a home, and a comfort to its owner. Naturally, however, lawns and gardens normally require very regular care, some of which can be expensive. You should be prepared to invest time, effort and money in any property which features lawns and gardens.

At the same time, a property with either no landscaping or landscaping in poor condition tends to demand even more time, effort and money than an already beautiful property. Look carefully at any property you consider buying, and ask yourself whether or not additional landscaping or lot improvements will be required. Factor the costs of that work into your total purchase price. In order to assess future landscaping expenses, ask yourself these questions:

- Is the property fully landscaped to your satisfaction? If not, how much landscaping work is required?

- If the property is fully landscaped, what is the condition of the lawns and gardens? Will extensive repair work be required?

- Do you already own the equipment you will need to maintain the current landscaping and/or the landscaping you intend to create on the property? If, for example, the lawns are large enough that you will require a gas powered lawn mower, and your current lawn mower is an electric model, you should account for the expense of new equipment when considering the total cost of buying the home.

Big Ticket Outdoor Items

Trees, shrubs and retaining walls are all examples of big ticket potential yard expenses. If the property you are interested in has a retaining wall, for example, you should inspect the wall very closely. Future repair or replacement costs can be very, very significant and, in certain instances, a retaining wall may have a grave impact on the value of your entire property.

While trees can certainly add charm and character to a property, they can also present special concerns which result in extraordinary costs. For example, trees and shrubs can block out desired sunlight from a home; if planted too closely to the house itself, trees and shrubs can cause a variety of moisture problems; and, in the later stages of life, large trees can present significant safety risks which are sometimes only alleviated by removal of the tree itself. The efforts and expense involved in taking down a very large tree (especially in urban areas where buildings are close by) can be enormous. On that note, let me tell you a tree story:

My wife and I once owned a property with several huge, magnificent trees in the backyard. As the biggest tree approached its 100th birthday, it was severely damaged by a Winter storm. Eventually, the tree deteriorated to the point where it visibly rocked in strong winds, threatening to fall on our neighbour's house or our own. Sadly, it had to come down. Cutting down a tree nearly 6 feet in circumference is, however, *not* a job for the amateur lumberjack - especially when the tree itself is growing in a narrow space between two houses. A tree removal *team*, with lots of equipment (including a boom truck) and $5,000.00 was all it took to remove that big, beautiful tree. Who would have guessed?

In order to avoid an experience like mine, ask yourself

these questions about trees, shrubs and retaining walls on the property:

- Is there a retaining wall currently on the property? If so, how old does it appear to be and from what has it been made? If the retaining wall required replacement or repairs in the future, would it be work that you could do yourself? What would be the potential cost of replacement or repair?

- Are all the shrubs and trees on the property a reasonable distance from the house and any other structures (sundecks, tool sheds, etc.)? If not, how will any resulting problems be corrected?

- Do any trees on the property (or on the property of a neighbour, for that matter) overhang the house or other structures on the property? If so, can any overhanging tree be easily accessed if removal (or even trimming) is required?

- Are the trees on the property young and healthy? Remember that every tree has a life span, and at the end of its life, it will likely have to be cut down. You should determine the cost of any tree removal in advance of purchasing the property.

- Are the trees on (or near) the property evergreens or deciduous? While this is a relatively minor consideration, you should remember that trees which lose their leaves each Fall *do lose their leaves each Fall*, and that could mean a lot of raking or leaf blowing for you. At that house we had with the massive tree, for example, my wife and I would rake an average of 60 bags of leaves off the lawn each year. If you are unable to do your own yard work (or strongly dislike it), a property with lots of deciduous trees may not be for you.

Fences and Sheds

A fence can be a useful component of any yard, particularly if you have children and/or pets. Aside from its utility, a fence can also add to the appearance of your yard. One of the cliché dreams of North American society is to have a family with a house and a white picket fence. Before you get too sentimental over fences, though, ask yourself what they will look like with peeling paint and rotten pickets. Unless you (and your neighbours) can live with that type of eyesore, it is important to consider the time and expense involved in maintaining a fence.

If a property you are considering as your next potential home *does not* have a fence, you should assess whether you will need one, now or in the future. As mentioned above, families with children and/or pets sometimes find fencing indispensable. This is particularly the case if the property is in a dangerous area (for example, near a river or lake, a cliff, a steep embankment, or a busy street). Before buying a property, decide if a fence is in your future; if you think the cost of *maintaining* a fence will be high, wait until you see the cost of *installing* one!

The same principles which apply to fences are also applicable to sheds. If you are considering the purchase of a property which has an existing shed, you must ask yourself whether the structure will require maintenance in the future and, if so, how much. If the property does not have a shed, think about whether one is necessary. Depending on the amount of storage space in the house itself, you may need a shelter for lawn care equipment and other items, such as bicycles, golf clubs, etc. Again, the only thing more expensive than maintaining an existing shed is likely the construction of a brand new building.

Some of the questions to be addressed regarding fences and sheds on a prospective property are:

- Is there a fence in existence? If so, how old is it? What is it made from? How much maintenance will it require? Further, you should ask yourself what it would cost to replace the fence at some time in the future.

- If no fence currently exists on the property, do you anticipate needing one? Again, the cost of constructing a fence should be factored into your purchase price.

- Is there an existing shed? If so, what is the condition of the shed? Is it sufficient for your needs? What costs will be associated with maintaining the shed? If no shed exists, will you be needing one? If you anticipate needing a shed, is there a location on the property for convenient construction? How much would it cost to build a shed?

Examining The House - From Outside to Inside

After having carefully inspected the property that accompanies any house, you will now be ready to think about the building itself. Aside from its curb appeal, the way the house looks when you pull up to the front door, many people don't bother with a really careful review of the building's exterior. The physical appearance of any house you buy is, naturally, important. More critical, however, will be the hidden costs of repairing and maintaining the outside of your new home.

Remember at all times that you should not trust your own inspection of a property, even if you have some background or experience in house construction. You should have an inspection conducted by a qualified individual. Even so, you should also take the time to examine all aspects of the property. On that note, some of the major points of examination should be:

The Foundation

You don't have to be an engineer to understand the importance of a foundation to the entire home structure. A house built on a bad foundation will be at risk of actual *collapse*. Well before the building collapses, however, its owner will almost certainly suffer from countless problems, including the curse of many badly constructed basements - *flooding*.

At this point, your inspection of the house is taking place *outdoors*. More comments on foundation inspections from *inside* the house are found on pages 38 to 48. Naturally, everything you want to know about the foundation of a house will not be visible on the outside; nevertheless, you *will* be able to make some important observations about the foundation structure, including:

- is the foundation constructed from poured concrete (i.e. one solid piece) or is it made from concrete blocks, bricks or stone? Foundations constructed from blocks, bricks and stones should automatically invite extremely careful investigation, since all of these items normally require use of mortar or some other adhesive material. When that material is weakened by moisture and frost, it can eventually shift or even disintegrate - leaving its owner with a nasty mess!

- if the foundation is solid, poured concrete, what is the condition of the concrete? Are there any cracks visible? If you are able to see cracks, how large are they and how are they positioned? Experts seem to agree that concrete will *always* crack somewhere. The question, though, is how many times the concrete in a foundation has cracked, how severe the cracks appear to be and what has caused them. In some ways, concrete can be compared to cake mixture. If mixed properly and allowed to cure (or bake) in perfect conditions, the result will be a great foundation (or cake!). If the concrete is not mixed properly, or if it is not cured in the correct manner, then it has a much higher prospect of turning out bad. Although you will not likely be able to properly judge the quality of the concrete used in a particular foundation, you should be able to see any severe symptoms.

Aside from the condition of the foundation itself, you should examine any windows which have been constructed in the foundation. Basement windows can be a source of flooding and even break-ins. If the house you are considering for your next home has a window or windows in its foundation, look carefully:

• does the window lie very near the surface of the ground? For that matter, is the window below ground level, in a window well? What is the condition of the window frame? Is there any obvious sign of rotting wood, breakage or recent replacement?

Once you have examined the exterior of a foundation, don't forget to look carefully at the top of the foundation on which the house rests. On occasion, holes and gaps will exist at this location, and could be a sign of a significant structural problem.

Before you shift your examination upward from the foundation, it would be wise to look at, and think about, the soil immediately next to the foundation. One of the big potential causes of foundation problems (including flooding) is poor drainage. In the worst cases of poor drainage, you may actually see puddles of water resting near the foundation of a house after a rain storm. In less obvious cases, the condition of the ground in the area of the foundation may provide some hints. For example:

- is the ground cold and damp, even on a warm Spring or Summer day? Is it extremely hard and dense? Is there moss growing nearby?

- on the other hand, is the ground next to the foundation too soft? For example, does your foot sink into the ground when you step on it?

- aside from soil, are there any other land conditions to consider? Are there concrete or stone walkways adjacent to the foundation? Is there a paved driveway adjacent to the foundation? In either case, are those surfaces slanted slightly away from the house, or would they carry surface water *toward* the foundation?

- where does the drain tile from beside the foundation lead? Drain tile is normally very important to a foundation because it *drains* water away from the foundation. If a house doesn't have drain tile, you should have the issue addressed by an expert, to make sure that no problem will result. Even if drain tile has been installed, look at the lay of the land from the house to the end of the drain tile: is the land sloped *away* from the house? Does the area where the drain tile empties seem unusually soggy? Does the area appear too flat to allow water to drain? If so, water may back up in the drain tile in storm conditions.

- what about eavestroughing? Is there eavestroughing

on all of the eaves? If not, you should make further en-
quiries. Without a system of diverting rain water away
from the house, you could face a higher prospect of basement moisture problems. Even if eavestroughing has
been installed, where does it direct the water? If rain
water empties out of the eavestroughing system right *at*
the foundation, for example, then a problem may exist.
On the other hand, if there has been an obvious effort by
a previous owner of the home to divert eavestroughing
water far away from the home, that too may be a sign of
past flooding problems.

Siding

You most often look at the siding of a house in respect
of aesthetics. Problems with siding may not be as obvious to
you if it *looks good* from a distance. In fact, some people would
be more tempted to purchase a house with beautifully-coloured
siding in poor condition than another house with ugly siding in
excellent condition. Some of the more obvious siding problems
will be identified through this series of questions:

- Is the siding made of wood or some synthetic material? If wood, what is the condition of the wood? Are all
  of the clapboards securely attached to the building? If
  painting is required, how significant will the project be?
  For example, has the existing paint begun to crack and
  peel to the point where extensive scraping efforts will
  be required? Further, how large is the house, and how
  accessible are its walls - especially at their highest points?
  The answer to these questions may determine if you will
  be in a position to paint the house yourself or if you will
  require the assistance of professionals.

- If the siding is made of synthetic materials, is it

paintable? If not, will the colour of the siding satisfy you (and your spouse, if applicable!) forever? Is the siding well secured to the house? Is it in good condition?

Windows

You will want to consider the type of windows which have been installed in the home, since window replacement (especially multiple window replacements) can be an expensive endeavour. Your thoughts on the windows of a house should cover a variety of potential concerns, including: heat efficiency, operational issues (do they open and close properly), maintenance; appearance and safety. These preliminary questions should help you assess a property's windows:

- Are the windows made of wood, aluminum or other metal? Are they paintable? If paintable, how difficult would it be to paint them? Would you require the assistance of a professional?

- Do all the windows open and close properly? Do they have window screens in place? Are all of the panes of glass in good condition? If the answer to any of these questions is no, you should determine what the potential cost of repair would be.

- Are there any obvious signs of heat efficiency problems? For example, are there any indications that a prior owner of the home has used plastic coverings to retain heat? (You *may* be able to see remnants of adhesive on the window frames for example.)

- Is there any sign of excessive moisture in the area of the windows (damaged paint or wallpaper, water stains on window sills, etc.).

- From a safety perspective, do all of the windows lock properly? How many windows are accessible from ground level? How many windows are hidden from view (under a sun deck, behind bushes, in a darkened walkway or facing a secluded back yard)? Keep in mind that windows present opportunity for home intrusion, and some windows may require expenditures for further security devices.

- In case of fire, are the windows large enough to provide for escape?

Roof and Eaves

A roof is an important component of any house, for obvious reasons. Once a roof is damaged, the homeowner is typically not in a position to delay repairs. Consequently, you should determine two things about the roof of any house you consider purchasing:

1. What is the condition of the roof *right now*? and

2. Regardless of the current condition of the roof, what would it cost to replace it in the worst case scenario?

Questions you should ask yourself about the roof of a home include:

- is the roof pitched or flat? If pitched, what materials have been used to make it? If the roof has been covered with shingles, are any shingles missing or damaged? Are the edges of any shingles curled? Do the shingles slightly overhang the eaves?

- if the roof is not covered by shingles, is the alternate material in good condition? Is there any sign of damage or rust?

- regardless of the material covering the roof, is there any sign of moss on the roof? Is there any debris on it (for example, branches)?

- if the roof of the structure is flat, is it made from tar and gravel? If not, is it made from a membrane system?

- in either case (pitched roof or flat roof) how is the roof drained?

- particularly in the case of a pitched roof, how steep is the pitch? If you live in a climate where snow is common, would snow or ice likely fall from the roof? You, a family member or a visitor to your home could be seriously injured by falling ice or snow if the issue was ignored.

- assume that any roof repairs will require the services of a professional contractor. Even so, are repairs to the roof likely to cost more than an average roof, due to either a steeper than normal pitch, or a flat roof system?

In addition to roofing questions, you should also ask questions about the eaves of the house. The eaves can impact on the condition of an entire building because they affect air flow and water drainage. Furthermore, eaves may have impact on your use and enjoyment of the home if they block too much sunlight or, conversely, allow too much sunlight into the house. The questions to ask yourself about eaves are:

- What are the eaves made of? Are they paintable or not? If paintable, would you be able to undertake that project on your own, or would you require the assistance of a professional?

- Are there vents visible in the eaves?

- Is there eavestroughing installed?

- What is the general condition of the eaves (recognizing that you may not be able to examine them carefully from ground level)? Are there visible gaps in the joints?

Stairs, Porches and Sundecks

Proper construction and maintenance of stairs, porches and sundecks can be very important as a means of protecting yourself against being sued. If a visitor to your home slips and falls because of poorly constructed or badly maintained stairs, you can be held liable for the victim's injuries. Additionally, repairs to items such as stairs, porches and sundecks are usually quite costly, and are quite often well beyond the ability of the average person. For all of these reasons, you should be fully aware of any defects in the entrance areas of a house before you buy it. Make sure you answer these questions:

- Are the steps to the home constructed of concrete or wood? In either case, are the steps in good condition (for example, are they cracked or broken)?

- Do the steps appear to have been properly constructed? Are they level and solid?

- Are handrails in place on all stairs?

- Do all steps have a slip-resistant surface?

- In the case of sundecks and porches, are they level and solidly constructed? How are they supported? Is the porch or deck surface far enough from ground level to allow ventilation?

- Are all decks surrounded by railings?

You should be aware of the fact that construction laws and local by-laws apply to all aspects of a property, and the same is true with respect to stairs, porches and sundecks. In fact, the building regulations which apply to these entrances are quite stringent, in order to protect the safety of pedestrians. An engineer or a qualified building inspector should be consulted to ensure that all applicable regulations have been met.

You have now finished a pretty thorough session of tire kicking on the outside of this property. If, eventually, you decide to make an offer to buy it, you will definitely want to hire home inspection experts to conduct a more thorough and proper investigation. For the time being, though, you will have at least considered some of the most major issues which could arise in the future of this home. Now it's time to go inside!

The Interior - Looking Past (And At) the Wallpaper

Many a home buyer has *agonized* over the cosmetic challenges of a house while, at the same time, walking blindly by major structural problems. As you tour the inside of any home, it will be important to think about the beautification projects that you will want to undertake - all of that work costs money, of course! *More* importantly, however, you will want to really pay attention to possible symptoms of major structural flaws.

In the end, you will be acting as the first line of your own defence against a nightmare house. *Experts, including a qualified home inspector and electrician, a plumber, a furnace specialist and more should be consulted before you agree to buy any house.*

For the moment, however, let's proceed with **your** interior inspection of the house. Since basements are frequently a source of *potential* headaches, start your inspection there.

The Basement

As you are proceeding down the stairs which lead to the basement, take your time to look around. What problems may the stairway pose for you and your family (or potential family) in future years? While conducting an initial viewing of a house, significant inconveniences may not be apparent, so you should imagine yourself trying to carry heavy and awkward pieces of furniture down the same set of stairs, using (or making usable) the stairs for frequent travel to and from a family room or other living space, and having young children or elderly relatives going up and down the stairs. Now, with all of those potential uses in mind, how does the stairway measure up?

Once you arrive in the basement, the nature and success of your examination will depend on several factors. Is it a fully or partially finished basement? Is the basement cluttered with the current owner's possessions? Is there enough light to actually see small details? You have to qualify the results of your examination based on these interferences.

The Unfinished Basement

An unfinished basement is, obviously, the easiest to thoroughly examine. Amongst the issues you should address are:

- The Floor - the construction of a basement floor will depend, in part, on the age of the house. Very old basements sometimes have dirt floors. You may be prepared to accept a dirt floor, but do so with the knowledge that it has its limitations, including a significant limitation when it comes to use of the basement as living space. Further, basements with dirt floors tend to be more prone to moisture and occasional infiltration of water, all of which will limit the use of the basement for storage purposes.

- If the floor of the basement is concrete, you will obviously inspect it for cracks. Keep in mind that the existence of cracks are not necessarily red flags of massive structural defects; instead, cracks in concrete are matters to note and discuss with an expert. That having been said, a concrete floor which is riddled with cracks is probably worth avoiding.

- Along the edge of the floor, where it meets the basement walls, you should look carefully for any sign of water infiltration. Sometimes, you will see water stains (which are usually white, powdery lines). Again, any sign of possible water leakage should be thoroughly investigated. A more obvious sign of potential water problems will be the existence of a small trench at the edge of the floor where it meets the basement walls. Very occasionally, a detailed-conscious builder from a previous era will have created such a trench as a precautionary measure to lead water towards a drain. More often though, the existence of trenching confirms a real flooding problem which may or may not have been fixed. In either case, trenching should be a red flag to you.

• You should also examine the basement floor for evidence of an existing or a previously existing sump pump. A sump pump is a device used to remove water from basements, and is installed in a hole in the basement floor. It is not uncommon at all for a home buyer experiencing flooding difficulties to find out that an existing sump pump had been hidden from his view (often behind moving boxes, sports equipment, and other storage items) before he purchased the house. For that reason, you should make sure that the basement has been thoroughly inspected *before* you commit to buying the home - including inspections behind (and under) storage items.

• Any posts which support beams and floor systems should comply with the local and national building requirements and, further, should be resting on some type of weight-distributing pad (whether concrete, steel or other acceptable system). While inspection of these most important structural issues, including support beams, posts and pads, are the domain of experts, your untrained eye *may* be able to identify obvious defects.

• *Walls* - the inspection of unfinished basement walls is similar to that of the floor. If the walls are constructed of material other than poured concrete, you may have quite a job on your hands! Basement walls constructed of concrete blocks, bricks or stone will have been mortared and, often, the mortar has a much different colour and texture than the blocks. For that reason, it may be somewhat difficult to identify sources of potential water leakages and block shifting. Nevertheless, you should examine the walls carefully, looking for symptoms of problems. For example, you may find water stains on the blocks themselves, or you may see evidence of patch work having been conducted on certain areas of a wall. Obviously, these observations would raise questions.

Walls constructed of solid concrete are, naturally, subject to the same cracking concerns that exist with respect to floors. Again, the existence of cracks may or may not be fatal to your interest in the house, and would have to be assessed with the assistance of an expert. However, you should look carefully at any existing cracks - *especially ones which appear to have been repaired!* Think of it this way; an unrepaired crack is more likely to be one which has not *posed* a problem (yet) for the current house owner. On the other hand, any crack which appears to have been repaired has obviously attracted someone's attention. A repair may have been attempted as a preventative measure, but it is more likely to have been the result of a previous water leakage. **You have to be very careful in the manner you address these cracks!**

Here is a scenario which is not uncommon in house transactions: a purchaser notices a crack in a foundation and asks for more information about that crack from the vendor. The vendor, in turn, writes a disclosure statement to the purchaser which indicates that the crack has been *repaired*, and there has been no water leakage from the crack *since the repair was made*. The purchaser buys the house with the false perception that the repair has fixed any water leakage problem. Months after buying the house, the basement floods as a result of the crack and the purchaser is left understandably irate. *Is there anything the purchaser can do in these circumstances?*

The answer, quite frankly, is probably no. In those circumstances, the buyer observed the crack before he agreed to purchase the house, and he had an opportunity to thoroughly investigate the crack for his own protection. He asked the vendor for information about the crack, and the vendor told him the truth, which was I (the vendor) experienced water leakage from the crack, I had it repaired and I have not experienced water leakage since. The purchaser did not ask any more questions. For example, the purchaser could have asked when the repair was made and by whom. The fact that the vendor did not experience any leakage *since completing* the repair does not mean that the repair was conducted properly or that it was effective.

If it became apparent that the vendor had lied to the purchaser in respect of the crack and its repair, or if the vendor had attempted to conceal the crack and previous leakage problems from the purchaser, *then* the purchaser would have a stronger legal claim to make against the vendor.

Other Elements of the Basement

Aside from the floor and walls, you will want to examine all other elements of the basement, including windows and window sills, exposed beams and floor joists, electrical wiring and components and plumbing components. Here is your homework in those regards:

- *Windows and window sills* - we have already confirmed that windows and window sills can provide very clear evidence of water leakages. If the windows are wooden, you should feel the window frame to determine if it is solid and dry. Anything less is probably cause for concern. Aside from the feel of the window frame, look for water stains or other evidence of moisture. Just as is the case with all other windows in the house, you should also assess the heat efficiency and the security of any basement windows.

- *Beams and Joists* - don't forget that the support beams and floor joists which are likely visible in the basement of a house play an important role in *holding the building up!* In some houses, these elements can look like (and be) the product of a do it yourself project. Needless to say, important structural components of a house should not be constructed by amateurs, and you may be able to identify potential concerns with beams and joists by simply looking at them. Eventually, you should ask a qualified expert to give you an opinion regarding the condition of these items but, for your purposes, it will be sufficient to simply eliminate houses which just should not be bought.

  Look for signs of rot and mildew on the beams and joists. Additionally, any signs of makeshift construction, uneven beams or joists, or beams not resting fully on support posts may very well be an indication of larger problems.

- *Electrical Components* - My wife and I once bought a house which had been built in the 1920's. For all of its charms (and there were many), the age of the house presented several significant drawbacks, one of which was the state of its electrical wiring. The basement of a house is often the best place to have a glimpse of the real condition of a home's electrical system, since at least part of that system is normally exposed. In the 1920's house that we bought, one could easily see ancient knob and tube wiring, which was used decades ago. White ceramic knobs held copper wires which were insulated with cloth and spelled, very clearly, F-I-R-E! While the electrical system did not prevent us from proceeding with the purchase of the house, my wife and I did so on the understanding that a major expense would be incurred in wiring upgrades.

You should look carefully at any visible wiring in the basement of the house you are examining. The wiring will lead to an electrical entrance. An entrance is not an inexpensive piece of equipment and, depending on the age and size of the one you are looking at, it may have to be upgraded. If that is the case, you should budget appropriately. It is also important to remember that the age of the entrance does not necessarily determine the age of the wiring throughout the house. Even if the entrance is brand new, all or part of the wiring (particularly that which is not exposed) may still be very old. For that reason, you should not gauge the age and the condition of the electrical wiring in a house by the age and condition of the entrance.

In the event that you purchase a house which must be re-wired, be prepared for the worst. In many houses, wiring is located in inaccessible areas, and replacing it can be gravely frustrating work. As you may imagine, aside from being time consuming and frustrating, it can easily end up being very expensive as well.

When you first look at a house, you may be so overwhelmed by its charm and character that practical issues (such as electrical safety) seem minimal. You may be tempted to say the former owner lived with the existing electrical system, so I should be able to do that, as well. Before you fall prey to that thought process, remember that old wiring may cause you to spend many long nights worrying about a fire or, at a minimum, may cause you the inconvenience of frequent power surges. *Ultimately, an outdated electrical system will cause you concern.*

• *The Plumbing System* - much of what was said regarding the existing electrical system in a house can also be
  said about the plumbing system. In the basement, you
  will probably have a clear view of sewage piping where
  it leaves the house and, as well, the pipes which carry
  fresh water into the home. Many newer buildings will
  be equipped with plastic piping and hoses, the latter of
  which are bendable and, in that regard, somewhat easier
  to replace than older-style copper tubing. In a home
  equipped with metal or lead sewage pipes and copper
  tube plumbing, you should be particularly interested in
  its capacity for future alteration. If there is even a prospect of needing an additional bathroom, for example,
  you will have to determine how adaptable the current
  system will be.
  Another problem which confronts many home buyers
  has to do with frozen pipes. You should attempt to determine whether or not any plumbing in the house runs
  along an outside wall. If the climate in which you live is
  cold in the Winter months (ie., below the freezing point),
  then you should think seriously about the prospect of
  pipes freezing - especially if they rest against, or in, a
  wall exposed to the elements. If you find pipes in that
  position, you will at least be able to make additional
  inquiries of a plumbing expert and, also, with the vendor of the home. You can be absolutely certain that, in
  the middle of an extremely cold Winter night, the last
  thing you will want to be doing is trying to thaw out a
  frozen pipe - or worse - cleaning up the mess after the
  pipe has burst!

The Finished Basement

A finished basement can be a real benefit for a home-owner. Having that extra living space is, at best, a convenience and, often, a necessity. When examining a finished basement, the walls, sub-floor and ceiling will prevent you from viewing many potential areas of concern. Since most (if not all) of the concrete is not exposed, its condition will remain questionable. The same will be true of the wiring and plumbing. While your home inspector may be able to identify concern in these areas, you should also ask for specific and written disclosure statements from the vendor.

In the inspection of a finished basement, it will be especially important to involve experts. Nevertheless, you can make some observations that will serve as red flags of potential problems. Consider these examples:

- *The Smell* - if a basement smells *funny*, you should be suspicious. Does it smell musty? If it does, that is probably a sign of moisture problems. Does it smell *too good* for a basement? Maybe the owner is trying to camouflage mustiness with strong deodorizers. Does the basement just smell *weird*? You may be experiencing a mustiness/deodorizer mixture. Again, a bad sign!
  Do not accept a brush off response to the effect that all basements smell musty! If the basement smells musty, it may have leaked in the past, or it may not be properly ventilated. Either way, something will have to be done to correct the problem, and that something could be simple or complicated.
  What if the basement has a strong, *pleasant* smell? Remember (and this applies to the inspection of the entire house) that many vendors try to appeal to your subcon-

scious with the smell of freshly baked bread, flowers or room deodorizer. Unless the kitchen of this house is in the basement, you should be at least mildly suspicious of any really strong aroma. More than once, vendors have attempted to mask odours related to basement dampness with scented candles, deodorizers, and more. Look around for the presence of deodorizers in the basement. Sometimes these will have been placed in very inconspicuous locations. If the vendor has gone to a lot of trouble in this regard, you should definitely ask yourself why.

Look Carefully - if a homeowner has a leaky basement *and doesn't want to tell you about it*, you have only a few ways to discover the problem yourself. As stated above, the smell of the basement may be a clue. How else may you expose a leaky basement, you ask? Answer these questions to find out:

- are baseboards and wood trim discoloured or stained? Is the gyproc or panelling discoloured?

- if there is carpeting in the basement, what colour is it? (A homeowner who *knows* that he or she has a basement leakage problem is less likely to install white carpeting, for example.) Is the carpeting in good condition? Are there any signs of carpet wrinkles or curls?

- does it appear that *everything* in the basement is being kept off the floor? What about electrical wires? Are they also arranged so that contact with the floor is minimal?

- if the basement has a sub-floor, does it feel solid or spongy?

- do you see any space heaters, fans, or other electrical equipment that may be used to dry out the basement?

Obviously, the inspection of a finished basement for signs of potential flooding is a difficult process and, for you, will involve considerable guess work. You may or may not uncover some causes for concern; the real inspection of the finished basement will have to be conducted by an expert.

A Look Upstairs

The main living area of a house is where many purchasers *start* to pay attention. Unfortunately, a good number of home buyers pay too much attention to the wrong things! As you know, people are often caught up in the excitement of a potential new home - imagining themselves *living* in the space. All of a sudden, cosmetic details can become more important than the practical concerns that *may* make the house a bad choice. **You must avoid the temptation of** *playing house*!

Remember that you are not the owner of this house yet; you are supposed to be *inspecting it* to decide if it deserves further consideration. The question of what paint colour would look best on the kitchen walls can be (and definitely should be) left to a later day. Your initial and primary focus has to be on the practical issues. As the old saying goes, "a two-bit horse dressed up with a ten dollar saddle is still a two-bit horse!"

In order to help yourself buy a great house, you will need to perform a great preliminary house inspection before involving your team of experts. Let's continue the process!

The Kitchen

As everyone knows, kitchens and bathrooms seem to attract the most renovation attention from homeowners. That fact is a hint that *you* may also want to renovate the kitchen of any home you purchase. The bad news is that kitchen renovations sometimes involve replacement of cupboards and other expensive work and materials. Ideally, it would be best to buy a house with a kitchen you like from the start. Here are some of the issues which have led to expensive kitchen renovations in the past:

- *Cupboard Space* - first of all, you may as well face the fact that, no matter how much cupboard space a particular house may have, *it will ultimately not be enough*! The only way you may possibly survive happily with limited cupboard space is if you are now (and remain forever) a bachelor or bachelorette. The best you can do in respect of the assessment of cupboard space is avoidance of obvious and major deficiencies.

  Look around the kitchen at the cupboards. Assess the amount of space available in relation to your own collection of pots, pans, dishes and counter top appliances. If already you have doubts as to whether or not this particular house offers sufficient kitchen storage space, ask yourself where more cupboards could be installed, and investigate how much that would cost. Aside from your pots, pans, cooking equipment and dishes, you will probably require some cupboard space for food - such as cans of soup and boxes of cereal. If the house has a built-in pantry for storage of canned goods and dry food, that will help.

  The next feature of the kitchen to think about carefully is the countertop. Is there enough open counter space to spread out a 20 lb turkey, a 10 lb bag of pota-toes and 4 types of vegetables? If not, you should seri-ously consider leaving immediately. While a limit on counter space may seem workable on your initial trip through the house, it will seem much less acceptable when you are rushing around trying to make a special dinner for a houseful of relatives. The problem with countertops is that finding space in a kitchen for more is usually difficult. Short of constructing an island in the middle of the kitchen, many counter-top starved home owners have been forced to make do with their frustrat-ing circumstances.

- *Table Space* - is this supposed to be an eat-in kitchen? Is there a dining room in the house as well? Depending on your answers to these two questions, you should measure the area of the kitchen reserved for eating in relation to the size of your family. *You must also take into account future additions to your family and occa-sional dinner guests.* If the kitchen affords barely enough space for a small table with two chairs, the problem is obvious; you will need extensive renovations! Figure these expenses into the total cost of the house.

- *Washing Dishes* - some home buyers do not make dishwashing a central consideration of their home in-spection. In my view, you need only to consider that, depending on the size of your family, this chore can con-sume a significant amount of time each day; further, and if the property does not already have an automatic dish-washer, you may wish to install one in the future. For these reasons, the kitchen must be assessed in the con-text of doing dishes. For example, is the sink located near the centre of the countertop? Is the sink large enough to handle lots of dishes? Is there a window above the sink? (People love to look out the window while they are washing dishes, you know!) Finally, how difficult would it be to install a dishwasher in the kitchen if necessary?

• *Appliances* - very often, home buyers negotiate with vendors to include the existing appliances in the purchase price. Again, this practice demands attention and planning from purchasers, because you must assess your own future needs against the existing condition of any appliances being thrown in to the deal. If the vendor's appliances are old, for example, you may as well budget to purchase new appliances in the next one or two years. If the vendor's appliances last you longer than one or two years, you can pat yourself on the back and be pleased with the great deal you negotiated. If, on the other hand, the vendor's appliances break down within your two year budget period, you will not be caught by surprise.

Remember, as well, that what may seem tolerable in the euphoria and excitement of the home *buying* process will undoubtedly seem substantially less acceptable in the relatively boring period of home-*living*. Any special characteristics of the vendor's appliances (such as their retro avocado colours or random clunking noises) may seem quirky and fun on the day of your home inspection; they will be more bothersome, though, when you own the house.

Bathroom(s)

Bathrooms are at the top of the renovation attention list with kitchens. As a departure from my general rule (to the effect that most cosmetic dislikes regarding a house should be considered on a *secondary* basis) I must admit that any grave concerns you have regarding the appearance of a bathroom should be added to your list of *primary* issues. The reason why cosmetic concerns in the bathroom can be important is that bathroom alterations are often as expensive as any renovations or repairs required in a home. The reason is simple: some bathroom colour schemes are very difficult to change on the cheap. For example, if you hate black toilets, and the house you are examining has a black toilet, one of the few options available to you is a complete replacement of that fixture. The same is true of 1970's-style tile. While some ceramic tile can be painted, you may easily be stuck with complete replacement - and tile replacement is not a fun (or easy) job! If the bathtub or shower stall is scratched and worn, there are, again, very few inexpensive repair options available. Basically, then, you should not take the view that you will try to grow into bathroom colour schemes or fixture problems that you hate at the outset.

Aside from those cosmetic issues, you need to inspect each bathroom for some of the common problems found in these rooms. First, look carefully at the ceiling and the walls. Do you see any sign of water stains or mildew? Do the walls themselves appear to be flat and level, or can you see evidence of bowing in any wall? Are there vents in the bathroom? Is it possible to determine where those vents lead (on this point, you will likely have to rely on other experts, but it is important to note that any bathroom fan or vent should draw moisture to the outdoors). Occasionally, the hoses designed for this purpose are not properly connected allowing moisture to collect in attics or other hidden areas of the house.

Check around any bathroom windows for signs of water leakage as well. Additionally, look under the bathroom sink for anything unusual, including damaged pipes, water and mildew stains and any evidence of past or present insect infestation. Yes, bugs! Some insects, such as cockroaches, earwigs and silverfish, are attracted to warm, damp areas. While your bug-scouting exercise will only identify an *obvious* problem, it is worth doing.

You should also look carefully at the faucets on the sink and bathtub. Again, your inspection will not reveal all of the potential problems in this area but *could* expose serious ones. For example, is there significant discolouration near the faucets, particularly anywhere from the base of the hot and cold water knobs to their tops? Quite often, faucets will leak anywhere that water can escape, and that leakage could be the sign of either a very minor problem (such as the need for a new rubber gasket) or a major problem (such as corrosion of the entire faucet unit). Finally, while you are looking at the bathroom faucets, you should determine if they are standard models. If replacement were necessary in the future, you should have some general idea as to the new type you would use. As long as you are not fussy, this should not amount to a major consideration. However, if you have always secretly lusted after some sort of special taps that you've seen in a friend's home or in a fancy hotel, remember that those taps may or may not fit the fixtures in your house and - even if they do - they may be expensive.

One final point on bathrooms: *be realistic in your assessment*! Consider the true needs of your family in respect of bathrooms, and don't settle on a house which can't meet those needs. You may have the temptation to say, "gee, having only one bathroom really won't work for the long term, but I can probably survive with it in the short term". If you chose to take this approach, remember that you should budget for your *actual* needs, which will involve renovation work. Furthermore, you should ensure that the house can accommodate your actual needs; for example, is there enough physical space in which to construct the bathroom facilities that you will need or want in the future? Can the plumbing system be revamped for that purpose? Can you afford all of that work? These are questions that should be asked *before* you proceed further with any interest in the house.

Other Rooms in the House

You would undoubtedly find it too tedious and repetitive if I made a list of questions and concerns for you to consider in respect of every additional room in a house. Many of the concerns you should have were listed previously; however, here is a list of general considerations to be applied in virtually every house examination.

- *Floors* - don't treat flooring as a detail unless you have a large bag of cash available to spend at your discretion. Flooring replacement can be expensive, particularly since most of us are not even remotely qualified for the job. Some observations you make about flooring in a house may be tolerable but others will not be acceptable at all, and you should be completely honest with yourself from the outset. If you really, *really* have your heart set on hardwood flooring in your living room or dining room, for example, think twice about buying a house that doesn't have it. Unless you can truly make do with what currently exists in the house, ask yourself if you have now (or will have in the near future) access to thousands of dollars for new flooring. If the answer is no, you may want to look for a different house altogether. The same is true with the condition of hardwood flooring (or any other flooring in the house, for that matter). If the previous owner of the house has kept several large German Shepherd dogs over the years, for example, and if those dogs have carved their paw prints into the flooring in a very noticeable way, you should obviously ensure that your budget will allow for flooring replacement before you go any further with your interest in the house.

Some further random thoughts regarding flooring: on several occasions over the years, I have had clients call me on the day of their house purchase to advise that their new house is infested with fleas. Now flea infestation is a crisis which, fortunately, can be resolved quickly by an exterminator. In those cases involving my clients, we were successful in recovering the cost of the extermination services from the vendor. Nothing, though, puts a damper on the excitement of moving into a new house as much as finding out it is full of tiny, vicious insects! For that reason, keep your eyes open for signs of pets in the house. If the owner has a cat or a dog, you may want to try this trick during your next review of the house. Wear white socks, and spend lots of time on the carpets in your sock feet. *Sometimes*, the fleas will actually appear on your white socks, and a couple of my clients have been successful in identifying flea infestations *before* buying their houses by using the white sock method. Realistically though, identification of flea infestation (or any other insect problems, for that matter) will require quite a bit of luck - white sock method or not. If you have any concerns about the presence of insects in the house, you should investigate further and, possibly, have an exterminator provide an assessment.

As a final point on flooring, look at the presence of any mats or rugs with suspicion. If you had a rip or burn mark in your vinyl flooring, or a huge dent in your hardwood, what would *you* do? The fact is that you would probably cover it up with a mat or rug! A vendor may be doing the same.

• *Walls and Ceilings* - in most houses, you will find that the walls and ceilings are in reasonable condition. Make sure you inspect each wall and ceiling carefully, however, to ensure that you have a good understanding of what work may be required if you ultimately buy the building. You may be able to obtain some hints from the age of the house itself. If the house is more than 20 or 30 years old, there is a much higher chance that the walls are constructed of plaster rather than gyproc. You have to be especially careful when purchasing a house that has plaster walls, as cracking can be very common and somewhat painstaking to fix. In all houses (but especially those with plaster walls), be suspicious of wallpaper. Wallpaper is sometimes used to hide significant imperfections in walls. Even if wallpaper has not been used as camouflage for cracks, you still have to take it into account in the event you will have any future desire to remove it. If you have ever stripped wallpaper, you know that it can be a brutal and frustrating project which, unfortunately, is menial enough that even the most unskilled of us will feel obligated to do it ourselves. In addition, most of the feelings expressed concerning wallpaper also apply in the case of panelling.

You will want to check for ceiling cracks in the same way you have checked for wall cracks. If a ceiling is made from tiles or some material other than gyproc or plaster, you should ask lots of questions as to *why* that is the case. Other than in the basement of a house, a drop ceiling may well be the sign of some problem, and that should be investigated. As you look at the ceilings, check for water stains, as well. Any brown discolouration may be an indication of previous plumbing problems. Aside from the obvious concern which arises from a possible plumbing leak in the ceiling, you should also recognize that such stains are troublesome when it comes time to repaint.

• *Closets* - sometimes, purchasers look through houses without really thinking of the way those houses would work for them. One of the things you may not notice about a house, for example, is the amount of closet space available. You can save yourself some grief by noting the number and sizes of the closets in the home, then comparing those closets to your existing storage space. Most houses built in the last 20 years will have similar closet allotments; for some reason, however, it is not uncommon to find older houses with much less available closet space. In any event, look over the closets with your needs in mind.

• *Furniture* - will your furniture fit in this house? For many purchasers (particularly first time buyers), the more relevant question is "how am I going to get enough furniture to fill this place up?" If you are in the process of buying a house, however, you likely have a considerable amount of your own stuff, and it is always nice to know ahead of time if your couch is too big for the living room or, worse, too big to fit in the door! You may have seen cases of people literally *jamming* bedroom sets, entertainment units or other items into very small rooms. Once again, the old principle holds true: these furniture woes are nothing that money can't fix. If you have lots of *extra* money lying around, your only concern should be whether or not one of your existing furniture items has sentimental value and can't be disposed of. If not, you will be able to buy yourself new furniture that *does* fit your home. Most of us, however, would not be newly furnishing a house immediately after purchasing it; instead, existing furniture would be used until replacement items could be purchased over time. If that is your situation, and if some of the furniture that you must make do with is definitely too large for the house you are looking at, you will have a tricky problem on your hands. Undoubtedly, it would be difficult to pass up a great house based on furniture issues, so just be aware of those issues in order to develop solutions.

• *Attic* - Many attics are simply not designed for easy-access inspection. In many homes, the attic is not use-able space. It is often little more than a crawl space, without even floorboards on which to crawl. If you are not a gymnast, but you are trying to inspect a crawl space attic, don't despair - you can still make some helpful observations before having a professional home inspector conduct a thorough analysis.

Unless there is lighting in the attic you will need a flashlight in order to make any observations whatsoever. In most cases, you will also need something to stand on (preferably a ladder), since attics are typically accessible by a trapdoor in a ceiling. Be prepared for a temperature change when you stick your head into the attic; normally an attic will be considerably hotter in Summer and colder in Winter than the rest of the house.

As I mentioned before, you will not be able to identify all of the potential problems which could exist in the attic. If, however, the attic provides very obvious causes for concern, you may well be able to see those issues before your building inspector arrives on the scene.

• For example: Is there any evidence of infestation by birds, bats or insects? Any of these visitors can pose a real nuisance in a house, and, more importantly, they present possible health risks. Bats can be particularly pesky, and getting rid of them is not a do it yourself job. Bats are not always willing to leave a home and, unless their means of entry is totally sealed, they may return before you know it. Furthermore, getting the bats out of the house is only part of the equation; their excrement poses a real health hazard and should be removed by a professional.

Apart from infestations, you should look carefully at the structure of the rafters in the attic. Does all of the wood appear to be solid? Are you able to see any water stains or signs of leakage? Do all of the joints where boards meet appear to line up properly? If an attic flush-roof system is very badly constructed, even a novice will be able to tell.

You should also look carefully at the attic insulation. A good insulation job should look quite uniform. A bad job may look a bit like patchwork. Furthermore, the insulation should not cover air vents in the eaves.

Even if you don't observe any of these clear no-nos in the attic, make sure it is inspected by a professional. The attic performs a number of important functions to the whole home, including insulation and ventilation.

The Kitchen Table

Why would you examine the vendor's kitchen table, you ask? Here's an idea that will save you time and expense if you proceed with purchasing the house, and which may tip you off to problems to cause you to avoid buying: when you make arrangements with the vendor to visit the home (either personally or through your real estate agent), ask that a series of documents relating to the house be left on the kitchen table. For example, ask the vendor to leave a copy of his deed, surveyor's certificate, annual heating bill statement, water and sewer fee statements (if applicable), property tax bill and electricity bill for your review. Additionally, consider asking the vendor to provide copies of any other documents which may be helpful to you in your assessment of the house, including: proof of recent renovations (if any), such as contractors bills; instruction booklets and warranties relating to air exchange equipment, heating equipment, pools, jaccuzzies, appliances; and documents pertaining to any other feature of the home. Ultimately, the vendor will probably be required to gather up these documents for whoever actually buys the house and, as a result, your request should not be viewed as unreasonable.

The benefit of having all of these property-related documents available to you at the time you inspect the house is that you will quickly be able to identify some major problems which would cause you financial hardship if you owned the house. For example, if the heating bills are extraordinarily high, you should ask more questions on that point and, also, inspect the house for heat efficiency concerns. The same is true of water and sewer charges. If the property taxes are too high for you, you should know upfront, so that you won't be surprised by the bill when it is too late. In other words, the vendor's paperwork demonstrating the cost of operating the house can give you a *sense* of what your costs may be as well. Keep in mind however that the vendor's living arrangements may be different than your own; for example, the vendor may have been able to withstand much cooler house temperatures than you can, or may have spent several months of each winter in a warmer climate. If either of those scenarios is true, the vendor's heating costs will not be a true reflection of your heating costs. Nevertheless, you should have some understanding of the home's operating costs before you proceed further with a potential purchase.

Similarly valuable information can be obtained from the vendor's deed and survey certificate. You may learn, for example, that an easement or right-of-way runs across the property to a neighbour's land. If that is the case, you will know in advance that someone other than you (or your invited guest) has a legal right to cross back and forth over the property, and that may not be acceptable. Furthermore, the surveyor's certificate may demonstrate encroachments - either by items owned by the vendor onto a neighbour's land, or a neighbour's items onto the vendor's land. An encroachment occurs when fences, shrubs, sheds or even houses end up wholly or partly on the other side of a property boundary line. In some cases, encroachments are not a major concern: sheds and some other items are relatively moveable and, therefore, encroachments caused by those units can be corrected. Some other encroachments are not easily corrected. For example, if the vendor's house is built partly on his neighbour's land (or vice versa) that type of encroachment is a major concern and requires immediate and serious consideration. Although you will need the advice of your lawyer and your land surveyor concerning any boundary or encroachment issues, having the opportunity to inspect the vendor's deed and surveyor's certificate may alert you to serious issues.

The reason you should ask for an opportunity to view proof of renovation work as well as instructions manuals and warranties for mechanical items is that those documents will give you either comfort or discomfort as to the quality of fundamental features of the house. While the vendor may boast of recent renovations to his house, you should be interested in knowing who the contractor was that conducted the renovations, and what the exact nature of the renovations was. If the vendor's documents establish that the renovations were conducted by a reputable contractor, and if the description of the work meets with the vendor's explanation of it, you will feel quite good; however, if the work was performed by a contractor with a bad reputation, of if the vendor has exaggerated the extent of the renovation work conducted, you will be suspicious.

The same type of consideration should be given to air exchange units, heating equipment, pools and large appliances. If the vendor cannot produce instructions manuals and warranties for these items, you should be aware of that in advance. Obviously, the fact that those documents are unavailable may not be fatal to your interest in the property, but it may have an impact on how much value you attribute to those features. In the course of reviewing the instruction manuals and warranties, you may also learn important information about the cost of operating the units and the amount of work involved. Again, none of this should cause you to lose interest in the property but it may change the amount of money you feel comfortable offering for the purchase of it.

Conclusion

Well, you have now inspected a house from top to bottom, inside and out. You should have a much better sense of the true condition of the house, along with the amount of repairs and renovations you are likely to require in the future. Initially, you should know that the house is able to meet your current needs as well as your potential future needs.

Do not assume, however, that your inspection of the home is complete; actually, your work should be only a preliminary step! Now your should know if you are interested in considering this house further. If not, you have saved yourself a lot of money and time in the form of further professional inspections and, more importantly, you have spared yourselves from the grief of owning an unacceptable property. If you are interested in proceeding further with this house, keep in mind that your inspection is not over; instead it has just begun! Now you have to involve one or more of the experts from your team to conduct thorough, professional inspections of the property.

A *proper* home inspection takes *a lot* of time, *a lot* of energy and at least some money. Making those investments *now* will definitely save you even more time, energy, money and grief during your years of home ownership.

The temptation of many home buyers is to approach the house inspection process superficially, paying more attention to cosmetic details than structural issues, and *hoping* that everyone else involved in the process will protect the purchasers' interests.

In the end, *you* are the person who stands to *win* or *lose* in your home purchase. For that reason, the ultimate responsibility for buying a great house is *yours*!

MAKE A GREAT AGREEMENT
OF PURCHASE & SALE

Too many home buyers are quick to sign an agreement of purchase and sale. After having trudged through more homes than can be remembered, and upon finally discovering a suitable property to purchase, the natural urge of the buyer is to sign whatever it takes to make that right house his own. Unfortunately, the agreement of purchase and sale is regularly thought of as being less important than it really is, and agreements are often signed hastily, without careful consideration.

An agreement of purchase and sale is viewed by many as a preliminary step in purchasing property. In fact, some buyers sign an agreement merely as an offer to purchase property, without seriously considering the consequences that will come about if the property owner accepts the offer. It is *critical* to recognize that the agreement is the most onerous and important legal obligation which most buyers ever incur. For that reason alone, buyers and sellers should give very serious consideration to the agreement and its contents. Additionally, buyers and sellers should recognize that an agreement of purchase and sale may be used to help one of them, or both, obtain special benefits and protection in the course of its transaction.

Since most agreements of purchase and sale are similar in their format, a detailed review of a standard form contract, as found below, will help in understanding issues which can be (and should be) addressed in the contract. Nevertheless, it is important for buyers and sellers to obtain legal advice before signing any agreement.

Analysis of An Agreement - Line by Line

Who is the purchaser?

Normally, an agreement of purchase and sale is initiated by a purchaser (i.e., the buyer). The purchaser commences the agreement of purchase and sale by making an offer to purchase the property for a particular price. The vendor (i.e., the seller) then has an opportunity to either (a) reject the offer, (b) accept the offer, or (c) make a counter-offer.

The purchaser should recognize that, by signing an agreement of purchase and sale, he is taking on legal obligations and *potential liabilities*. For example, once the purchaser has made an offer to purchase the property on particular terms, the vendor can accept the offer and create a binding contract. At that point, the purchaser is *required* to complete the contract, unless some other event occurs which allows the purchaser to avoid his obligations. Consequently, the purchaser should realize that he could be sued by the vendor if he did not complete his obligations under the agreement of purchase and sale.

The purchaser should also recognize that completion of his obligations may not be entirely within his control since, in most cases, he is relying upon a team of individuals, including his banker, his lawyer, his surveyor, his home inspector and the vendor to assist him in the completion of the purchase according to the contract terms. If, for example, the agreement cannot be completed because of a flaw in title of the property, which flaw prevents the purchaser's bank from providing the mortgage funds necessary to buy the property, then, conceivably, he would be unable to complete the transaction.

In some cases, the purchaser's failure to complete his purchase of the property can result in a lawsuit by the vendor. The vendor may be able to sue the purchaser for damages caused by the cancelled sale. The damages which the vendor may incur as a result of the failed contract would probably include any difference between the price at which the vendor had agreed to sell the property to the purchaser and the price which the vendor eventually obtained for the property from another buyer. The vendor may also be entitled to damages for interest which the vendor would have earned on the money which the purchaser had agreed to pay to the vendor, along with bank charges which the vendor may have to pay because the purchaser did not buy the property on the date which he agreed to buy it. Since the purchaser can be held liable for failing to complete the agreement, *careful thought should be given as to who should sign the agreement for the purchaser.*

If more than one person is intending to purchase the property (such as a married couple), it is normally prudent for both of them to be named as purchasers, and to sign the agreement as such. In that way, each of the purchasers would accept the legal obligations arising from the agreements and would conceivably split any liability which would arise if the agreement was not completed. The sharing of liability may, however, be a good reason why only one eventual owner may best be the sole purchaser named on an agreement. Two business partners, for example, should *consider* having only one sign the agreement. Normally, if the agreement is not completed, then, both partners would be on the hook against the vendor, and both partners would incur legal obligations arising from the agreement.

On the other hand, circumstances may arise when only one purchaser executes the agreement. For example, if the agreement is risky and potential liability is high, great care should be taken to consider the legal ramifications which would arise if the agreement failed. A purchaser may wish to protect other parties from the possibility of a lawsuit and, in that event, the purchaser who should be named in the agreement may be the purchaser who is able to most effectively handle the liability. The case of a commercial property serves as a reasonable example: if a small convenience store owner wishes to purchase a second store, she may do so in her own personal name or, alternatively, in the name of a company she has incorporated to operate her first store. If the owner names herself individually as the purchaser, she accepts *personal liability* for any consequences of the agreement. On the other hand, the store owner may wish to name her company as the purchaser so that any liabilities arising from the agreement fall to the company. If you have options available to you, get some legal advice as to the pros and cons of each one *before* you sign an agreement.

Who is the vendor?

As has been stated previously, the vendor is the seller of the property. *The vendor named in the agreement should be the actual owner of the property.* Unfortunately, you may not be unable to confirm, at the time you make an offer to purchase a property, that the vendor is the actual owner of the property. Normally, a clause appears in a standard form of contract to confirm that the vendor *must be* the owner of the property in order to make the agreement valid. Nevertheless, a purchaser should make some inquiries to determine ownership of the property and, if the vendor appears to be married or to have a common-law spouse, it may be worth while to name that spouse as the vendor, as well.

The same potential liabilities apply to the vendor as to the purchaser. If the vendor fails to complete her obligations under the agreement, the purchaser may have an opportunity to sue her for damages, or even *specific performance* (actual completion of the sale). Consequently, the vendor should carefully consider the terms of the agreement before signing, to make sure that the agreement can be completed.

Buy the Right Property

A standard form contract will normally provide a space to write in the location of the property, which is normally stated as its civic address. The civic address should be stated accurately on the agreement in order to avoid any confusion as to the property's location.

Additionally, a standard form contract may provide for a legal description of the property, which should be completed in as much detail as possible. A real estate agent or a lawyer can be of assistance in this regard. If the property is a subdivided lot which has been registered in the local registry office, it may be sufficient to state the lot number and the number of the plan on which the lot appears as its legal description. If, however, the property is not a subdivided lot, it may be more prudent to attach the legal description from the vendor's deed as a schedule to the agreement, and to refer to the schedule on the face of the agreement itself.

The importance of describing the property in as much detail as possible is that it may prevent later confusion, or alleged confusion, between the purchaser and the vendor. A clear description of the property makes it difficult for either party to allege that he or she believed the property which was to be purchased, or sold, was different than the one described. For that reason, both parties should ensure that their understandings of the property are the same.

Amount of the Deposit

The deposit is the amount of money which the purchaser pays to the vendor, in advance, to confirm the agreement to purchase the property. The deposit ensures the vendor that the purchaser is serious about buying the property and, additionally, the deposit serves as consideration for the agreement itself. A standard form contract will normally state that the deposit is to be returned to the purchaser if the agreement is not completed at the fault of the vendor. If, however, the agreement is not completed because of the purchaser's fault, the deposit normally is surrendered to the vendor. Unless specifically stated, the payment of the deposit to the vendor because of a breach of the agreement by the purchaser does not end the purchaser's liability to the vendor. Consequently, *the purchaser may forfeit the deposit and also be subject to a lawsuit by the vendor.*

A deposit is often held for a considerable length of time, until the closing of the real estate transaction. For that reason, the purchaser should attempt to negotiate the smallest deposit possible; naturally, however, the vendor will prefer to receive a larger deposit, and negotiation in that regard can be quite important to both sides.

What's Title, and Why Examine It?

Title is essentially the legal ownership of the property. Only someone who has good title to the property is able to legally transfer it to a buyer and, therefore, it is absolutely critical for you, as the purchaser, to ensure that the vendor of the property has good title to the property. The last thing a purchaser wants to learn is that a vendor does not actually own the property, or that someone else has a claim against the property.

The purchaser should definitely hire a lawyer to search the title to the property and to certify that the vendor has good title. The title search procedure involves a review of the records at the registry office in the jurisdiction where the property is located. Presumably, a document has been registered each time that the property has been sold or mortgaged, so that the history of the property's ownership may be followed from the time that it was granted by the King or Queen of England through to the present date. The purchaser's lawyer should ensure that the property has always been sold properly, so that no one else has a valid claim of ownership.

Many jurisdictions have adopted a land titles system which makes proof of land ownership much easier than it used to be. If you do not live in one of those jurisdictions, or if the property in question has not been registered in the system, be particularly careful. As may be imagined, a title search is often very tedious and complicated work. Often, piles of dusty old records (some of which may be handwritten) must be read and examined from a legal perspective. The purchaser should, therefore, stipulate on the agreement that he requires as much time as possible to have the title searched and to make requisitions against it. (A requisition is simply an objection, or a challenge, to the vendor's ownership).

Once the purchaser has made a requisition, it is the vendor's responsibility to correct the problem which has given rise to the objection. If the vendor does not resolve the problem, the purchaser may cancel the agreement - provided the agreement allows it. A period of at least thirty (30) days is normally preferred for the conduct of a title search.

While a search may be completed much more quickly, the more time reserved for it the better. On that note, it is equally important to make certain that the purchaser's lawyer obtains the final agreement as soon as possible. Sometimes, miscommunication between purchasers and their real estate agents results in a delay in getting the agreement to the purchaser's lawyer. The lawyer will not be able to commence a title search until the Agreement is received and, therefore, the purchaser should personally confirm delivery of the agreement to the lawyer.

Similarly, a standard form agreement will usually require the purchaser and the vendor to stipulate the length of time that the vendor will have to rectify any title requisitions made by the purchaser. Actually, requisitions are normally made by the purchaser's *lawyer* and answered by the vendor's *lawyer*, often with very limited involvement of the purchaser and vendor themselves. Nevertheless, the lawyers will need time to resolve any title problems, since it is sometimes necessary to locate past owners of the property and to obtain written declarations from them regarding the history of the property's ownership. Occasionally, it may be necessary for the lawyers to present a title problem to a judge, so that a decision may be made as to whether or not the requisition is reasonable or, alternatively, to determine who is the actual owner of the property. In some jurisdictions, court procedures allow problems of this nature to be heard by the courts quite quickly. The time necessary to correct a title problem can be significant, though, and ten days is not excessive if the parties really want to solve any possible title problems. The purchaser may wish to abandon any purchase of a problem property, however, and he can gain more control of his fate if he limits the vendor's time for a response to five days.

A purchaser should recognize that the length of time agreed upon for the correction of title defects will be the length of time that he or she will be delayed in purchasing the property. If the agreement affords ten days to the vendor to rectify any title defects, the purchaser is bound to wait that period of time *just to find out if the problem can be fixed*. If the problem has not been corrected at the end of the stipulated period, it is likely that the vendor can repay the purchaser's deposit funds and consider the agreement null and void. The purchaser, on the other hand, would have effectively lost ten days from his or her schedule - with no compensation. For that reason, purchasers may want to keep requisition periods short.

Conversely, a vendor should attempt to obtain as much time as possible for the rectification of title defects. The vendor will not want to have the agreement cancelled because of a title defect, so he or she would first negotiate with the purchaser for an extended period in which to resolve any problems raised by the purchaser's lawyer. Sometimes the vendor will recall if his or her lawyer raised any issues of concern at the time the vendor purchased the property. If the vendor's lawyer had found a problem when the property was purchased, chances are good that the same problem will surface at the time of the sale. Even if absolutely no problem had surfaced when the vendor purchased the home, the vendor may feel more comfortable in accepting a shorter period of time for the rectification of title defects. In either case, the vendor can gain a better sense for the potential of problems being raised simply by talking to the lawyer who represented the vendor on his or her purchase of the property.

Date of Completion

The agreement of purchase and sale should stipulate the date for completing the transaction. Most standard form agreements will indicate that the transaction may be finalized on or before the date for the closing.

The closing date is of more *practical* than *legal* concern to the parties. Obviously, both parties will have to move their entire households and the vendor, particularly, will have pressure to ensure that the house is vacant on the date of closing. Both parties should, therefore, consider all of the things to be accomplished between the making of the agreement and the closing date, and enough time should be allotted to permit a comfortable move.

Vacant Possession

An agreement of purchase and sale should stipulate that vacant possession of the property is to be given to the purchaser on the closing date. Basically, vacant possession means that the vendor is to have removed all of his belongings from the property, and is to have totally vacated the premises. The purchaser should insist on this type of provision, and should ensure that it is met since, otherwise, it is impossible to fully inspect the condition of the property before buying it. If, for example, the purchaser completes the transaction before the vendor has completely moved his possessions from the property, any damage caused by the vendor in the completion of his move may be difficult to recover. Sometimes, the vendor will accidentally dent a wall or break a window while he is removing his furniture from the house. If the transaction has not been completed, the purchaser can, at least, request a holdback of some of the purchase money until the problem has been fixed by the vendor. If the damage caused by the vendor were a broken window, for example, the purchaser may insist on a holdback of the amount estimated to repair the damage and, if that were the case, the purchase price would be paid to the vendor's lawyer, less the estimated window repair costs. The vendor and purchaser would then agree as to who would repair the damage; normally, the purchaser will feel more comfortable if he repairs the damage himself, and would use the holdback money for that purpose.

One exception to the requirement of vacant possession occurs when the property contains a rented apartment. Laws prevent landlords from evicting tenants in certain circumstances, and evictions usually require notice periods before the tenants can be forced to leave. Consequently, the tenant in the property may be permitted to stay in the property, even after the closing date. If that is the case, the purchaser should ensure that the residential tenancies legislation has been met by the vendor, so that the tenant does not have any cause for complaint or legal action against the *purchaser* as a result of the vendor's actions or inactions.

If a tenant is going to remain in the property, it is critical for the purchaser to address the question of *the lease*. While having a tenant may be valuable to the purchaser, the value can be completely negated if an unfavourable lease exists. As one example, if the existing lease required you (as landlord) to provide the tenant's heat, you will be very frustrated if the heating costs go through the roof - especially if you think the tenant is being wasteful. The much better approach is to make a new lease (in writing), if possible. Further, the purchaser should determine the whereabouts of any security deposit provided by the tenant to the vendor, and should ensure that the security deposit is properly turned over to the purchaser at the time of the sale. *Finally*, and in relation to tenants of the property, the purchaser should ensure that any rents collected by the vendor before the time of closing are adjusted, so that the purchaser gets the benefit of the rents from the time that he actually buys the property.

Adjustments?

The agreement will probably stipulate that a number of cost issues will be adjusted for the date of closing. Taxes, water rates, local improvements levies, tenant's rental income and similar issues are the normal subjects of adjustments.

If property taxes are charged on a yearly basis, for example, and if the vendor has already paid the property taxes for the year in which the transaction occurs, then the vendor will want to recover part of the property tax money which he has already paid. In that event, the amount of the property tax paid should be divided by the number of days in the year and multiplied by the number of days left for the purchaser's ownership of the property. If you, as the purchaser, buy the property on December 1st, therefore, you will own the property for 31 days of that year and should pay 31 days of the property tax.

A similar adjustment should be made in respect of other applicable charges and benefits. In the case of oil heat, however, the normal practice is to have the vendor fill the heating oil tank on the date of closing, and to provide a receipt for the oil to the purchaser's lawyer. You, as the purchaser, would then pay the vendor for the full tank of heating oil. Since the cost of a tank of heating oil can sometimes be several hundreds of dollars, you may wish to avoid that cost at the time of closing, recognizing that it will, nevertheless, come up in the near future. You can sometimes negotiate with the vendor to avoid the purchase of a full tank of heating oil, but the risk in doing so is that the house will be left without heat before the purchaser is able to order and obtain more fuel. Depending on the time of year, the consequences of this development could be grave.

Representations

Standard form agreements of purchase and sale often stipulate that no "representations, warranties, collateral agreements or conditions" affect the agreement, except as have been expressly stated in writing. This type of clause is often overlooked, and is almost always underestimated. All parties to an agreement of purchase and sale should carefully consider the ramifications of exclusionary language, since it could easily negate the legal effect of any assurances, or side agreements, made by the parties. If, for example, you were to specifically ask a vendor about the condition of his property, and if the vendor indicated *verbally* that the property was in great condition but, on a disclosure statement, indicated that he did not know the condition of the property, then you may have difficulty in taking any legal action against the vendor based on his *verbal* misrepresentation.

As a purchaser, you should, therefore, ensure that any statements which the vendor has made about the condition of the property are put in writing and provided with the agreement. Standard form disclosure statements are sometimes incorporated into standard form agreements, and there is a very strong temptation for most purchasers to accept the wording of these standard form disclosure statements. While the effect of disclosure statements is explored more deeply in the following pages, a discussion of representations in general is an appropriate time at which to acknowledge the significance of disclosure documents. If you are a purchaser, and you want to be certain that the vendor is providing you with accurate information about the property, *you should not rely on any statement which the vendor will not make in writing.* You should also read any written statement provided by the vendor, to make sure that it has not been watered down by qualifications. One qualification which regularly appears in disclosure statements is that the information provided is correct "to the best of the vendor's knowledge and belief". If a statement made by the vendor under that qualification proved to be wrong, the purchaser would have difficulty in claiming damages from the vendor as a result of the misrepresentation, since the purchaser would have the onerous job of proving that the vendor actually *knew* and believed that the statement was false. An unqualified statement, on the other hand, is easier to prove incorrect. Consider the following examples:

1. "To the best of the vendor's knowledge and belief, the house does not contain UFFI"; and
2. "the house does not contain UFFI."

After buying a house, a purchaser who found UFFI in it would expect the vendor to pay for the cost of removing the material. If you, as the purchaser, had accepted the disclosure statement marked "1", you would first have to prove that the house actually contained UFFI, and *then* you would have to prove that the vendor knew (or ought to have known) that the UFFI was present in the building. Even if you *suspect* that the vendor knew about the UFFI, that knowledge may be extremely difficult to establish. Since the vendor may not have had any reason to remove siding from the house or to otherwise inspect the insulation, you may not even be able to show that the vendor was aware of any insulation at all (let alone UFFI) in the house. If you could prove that the vendor was aware of the presence of some insulation, you would still have to establish that the vendor recognized the insulation as UFFI. Obviously, in this scenario you would have significant difficulty in proving your claim against the vendor.

Had you insisted upon the Disclosure Statement marked "2", your claim against the vendor would be more easily proved. Simply put, in the second situation you would, conceivably, be required to prove only that the house did contain UFFI.

The prudent purchaser will, therefore, carefully consider the representations, warranties, collateral agreements and conditions which he wishes to rely upon in the Agreement, and will ensure that all of these matters are properly and effectively reduced to writing.

Just as the purchaser should insist that all of the terms of the agreement be put in writing, the vendor should make a similar demand. Since an agreement on paper is more likely to be clear, and less likely to be selectively expanded or edited to suit the needs of one of the parties, both sides will benefit from the certainty afforded by a written agreement. Nevertheless, the vendor should not take his obligations under any such written document lightly; if any representation is made in a disclosure statement or otherwise, the vendor should be certain that the information in his statement is correct. The vendor should not, therefore, guess at any information or rely on information which has been previously provided to him. If he does not actually know whether or not the house contains UFFI, for example, he should state that fact. Any guesses or carelessly made statements may easily come back to haunt the vendor.

The good news for both vendors and purchasers is that home inspectors are normally capable of alerting prospective home buyers to possible problems with the property. The vendor may refuse to provide representations to the purchaser, and instead insist on having the buyer inspect the property and come to his own conclusions about its condition. By doing so, the vendor virtually ensures that the principle of *caveat emptor* (let the buyer beware) is applicable to the transaction. The purchaser is then left with the onus of satisfying himself as to the condition of the property and, if he wishes to do so, he can hire a home inspector to provide him with a written report on its quality. If the home inspector misses problems that later become evident, the purchaser can conceivably sue the home inspector for his error. In this day and age, it should come as no surprise that the best advice to both parties is GET IT IN WRITING!

The Risk Until Closing

As discussed previously, a period of time should separate the signing of an agreement and the actual property transaction. During this period, the purchaser has a chance to conduct a title search, while the vendor has an opportunity to vacate the premises. An important (but obscure) question applicable to this situation is: "Who should insure the property, and bear the risk of any damage to it, before closing?" Most standard form agreements of purchase and sale stipulate that the vendor will bear the risk of the property until the closing date and, further, that the vendor will keep the property insured until closing. Although the vendor is normally obligated to keep the property insured, the Vendor would (in the case of a fire or other disaster) maintain any insurance proceeds in trust for both parties until the purchaser decided if he wanted to complete the purchase and accept the insurance proceeds as part of the transaction or, alternatively, cancel the agreement and have his deposit returned.

As one may have guessed, it does not often occur that a property is destroyed in the short period of time between the signing of an agreement and the closing date. The fact is, however, that a disaster can occur and, if no stipulation has been made in the agreement as to the apportionment of risk, the parties may end up in an argument as to whether or not the transaction must be completed. Except in rare circumstances, a purchaser will not want to purchase the charred ruins of his new house. Occasionally, however, the purchaser may be most interested in the property itself, and not the house, and may want to complete the transaction in order to obtain the land. Most likely though, the purchaser will take a second opinion under the agreement, and will accept the return of his deposit and the cancellation of the transaction.

The vendor, on the other hand, may wish to sell the property regardless of its condition. While it would be somewhat unreasonable for the vendor to expect the purchaser to buy a burned out home, the vendor would argue that he had already made plans to move into a new house and, with his transfer of the remaining property and the insurance proceeds to the purchaser, the transaction should be completed.

Since the vendor remains in possession of the property during the period between the signing of the agreement and the closing date, it seems more fair that the vendor be required to bear the risk of the property until the transaction is completed. The vendor is more likely to take care of it if he knows that the transfer may not be completed after the occurrence of a disaster. Further, the vendor would probably have the property insured at the time the agreement was made, and it would be simpler for the vendor to continue the insurance until the closing date.

Expiry

Often, the agreement document is used by a purchaser as a means of offering to buy the vendor's property. For example, if the vendor has listed his property for sale at the price of $90,000.00, the purchaser may not want to pay that amount, but may offer a lower price. In that case, the purchaser may decide to complete an agreement of purchase and sale at a price less than $90,000.00, at which time the purchaser delivers the agreement of purchase and sale to the vendor for his review. The vendor has not agreed to accept the reduced purchase price at this point and, consequently, the purchaser's agreement of purchase and sale is actually an *offer* to buy the property from the vendor at the reduced price. The vendor must decide whether or not he will accept the reduced price from the purchaser and, if he does so, he must sign the agreement so that it becomes an actual agreement as opposed to a mere offer.

Because an agreement is usually an offer when it leaves the hands of the purchaser, standard form agreements of purchase and sale may stipulate the length of time that the offer will remain available to the vendor for acceptance. A standard form agreement of purchase and sale may stipulate that:

"This offer shall remain irrevocable by the purchaser until _____
on the _____ day of _____,
20____, after which time, if not
accepted, this offer shall automatically become null and void,
with all deposit money returned
to the purchaser without interest."

A clause of this nature works to the benefit of both the vendor and the purchaser. The vendor benefits because he knows the length of time he has to consider the purchaser's offer without having it revoked. If no timeframe were stipulated in the offer, it could be *revoked* by the purchaser just as the vendor was making the decision to accept it. The stipulated timeframe allows the vendor to seriously consider the offer without the pressure that may affect his decision if he was forced to worry about an unexpected withdrawal of the offer by the purchaser. Conversely, the clause is of benefit to the purchaser, because he knows how long he is obligated to wait for a response from the vendor before he can consider the offer rejected. If the purchaser does not receive an acceptance of the offer (i.e. the agreement signed by the vendor) by the time stipulated by the duration clause, he may then consider his legal obligations finished and may proceed to look at, and possibly offer to purchase, other properties.

Purchasers sometimes attempt to use the duration clause as a means of applying pressure to the vendor. Purchasers attempt to accomplish this by making the time frame for accept-ance of the offer very short. While this strategy may sometimes benefit the purchaser, it is more frequently a pointless charade which benefits neither party. Unless compelling reasons exist to do otherwise, the purchaser should afford the vendor *at least* 24 hours to consider the purchaser's offer. Even if the vendor does not accept the offer, he may issue a counter-offer to the purchaser, which would still allow the purchaser to buy the property at a price less than the original price set by the vendor but more than the purchaser's offer. A counter-offer would appear on a standard form agreement, which normally includes spaces specifically for that purpose. If a counter-offer is made by the vendor, the process starts all over again, with the purchaser then having an opportunity to consider the counter-offer before deciding to accept it or reject it. Sometimes, the offer and counter-offer negotiations are repeated several times before a deal is struck between the purchaser and the vendor.

The Serious Effect of the Contract

A standard form agreement may indicate that the purchaser's offer, as it appears on the document, becomes a binding contract between the vendor and the purchaser when the offer is accepted by the vendor. While this provision may seem to be a statement of the obvious, it does confirm that both parties intend to be bound by the agreement, and that they recognize it as a legal obligation to purchase (and to sell) the property.

Further, a standard form agreement may stipulate that the contract shall be binding on the "heirs, executors, administrators, successors and assigns" of the purchaser and vendor. If a stipulation of that sort is made, the parties should recognize that, not only are they personally obligated to complete the agreement, their *estates* would be obligated to carry through the transaction if either the purchaser or vendor were to die before the closing date.

Conditions

A critical aspect of any agreement is the clause containing conditions stipulated by the parties. The current practice is to attach a "Schedule A" to the agreement of purchase and sale, which contains a list of various conditions which the parties must meet in order to complete the transaction. The purchaser, particularly, will want to ensure that certain conditions are made a part of the agreement.

If, for example, the purchaser does not have the full price of the property in his bank account when he first signs the agreement, he should ensure that a financing condition is included. A first-time home purchaser may be required to borrow as much as 95% of the purchase price and, if that is the case, he should stipulate that the agreement is conditional upon his ability to obtain satisfactory financing, in the required amount, from his bank. The financing stipulation should be worded so that the agreement becomes void if the purchaser is unable to obtain the necessary financing. Otherwise, the purchaser will be left in the extremely difficult position of having a legal obligation to complete the agreement, but not having the financial means to actually do it. *The importance of the financing condition cannot be underestimated.*

Another common condition which is included by purchasers in an agreement is a requirement for a satisfactory inspection of the property. Since many purchasers have no expertise in home construction, electricity, plumbing and similar matters, it is prudent to have an expert review the property for deficiencies before actually buying it. If the purchaser does not include an inspection condition in the agreement, he may be bound to buy the property even if he learns that the house is slowly (or quickly) falling down. An inspection condition should stipulate that the agreement is conditional upon the purchaser obtaining a satisfactory inspection report from a property inspector of his choice. If the property inspector uncovers problems with the house, the purchaser should be able to recover his deposit and cancel the agreement. The vendor, however, should limit the length of time that the purchaser has to conduct his property inspection. If the purchaser has not concluded his property inspection within a reasonable time (say, for example, 7 days), then his right to do so should lapse. Otherwise, the vendor is stuck waiting for the purchaser to complete the inspection which ultimately may not be satisfactory and, if not, the purchaser can cancel the agreement and cause the vendor to lose valuable time in the sale of his property.

If the property is not serviced by a municipal water and sewerage system, the purchaser should insist upon a satisfactory water potability test and an inspection of the septic system. A property which is not serviced by a municipal water and sewerage system obviously draws its water from a well. The quality of the water from the well is critical to the purchaser, since poor quality water can cause severe inconvenience and considerable expense to the purchaser. A water potability test involves testing the water for coliforms (basically, unhealthy contamination). If the well water contains unacceptable levels of contamination, it may be necessary for the owner of the property to perform expensive repairs on the well, or, alternatively, completely replace the well. If a new well has to be dug on the property, it may be that all of the property is contaminated and no uncontaminated water is available. The purchaser must, therefore, ensure that the agreement contains a condition that the well water meet acceptable standards.

Unfortunately, many standard form agreements contain a standard form condition that well water meet or exceed Department of Health Standards. While Department of Health standards will confirm that the water is suitable for human consumption, they do not judge some other critical water qualities, such as iron content. The well water may, then, be suitable for human consumption but, ironically, unsuitable for use in laundry and household cleaning functions. Large quantities of iron bacteria in well water may oxidize when exposed to air, producing a rust-coloured tinge which can stain clothing, bathroom fixtures and dishes. Other minerals, including sulphur, can cause your water to smell badly as well. A purchaser may wish to expand the typical water quality condition to include satisfactory testing for iron and all other minerals and particles.

A septic system is more difficult to test. If the property in question is not serviced by a municipal sewerage system, it probably has a septic field under the front or back yard. Sewage from the house runs out of the house to a septic tank which is buried underground and, after nature has broken down the sewage with the help of the septic tank, the residue flows into the septic field and is filtered through gravel until it is released back into the earth. A poorly installed septic system will cause a multitude of problems including plumbing backups and, occasionally, the escape of sewage above ground. Any of these problems can be very traumatic to a purchaser, and can result in significant repair costs. A purchaser may, therefore, wish to stipulate that the agreement is conditional upon a satisfactory inspection of the septic system, including a review of all installation permits and inspection reports prepared by government authorities. With that in mind, it may be necessary to ensure that the vendor will *assist* the purchaser in obtaining information from the government with respect to the septic system.

Another clause which is worth noting in the conditions is a requirement that the vendor provide disclosure of issues important to the purchaser. One of the most frequently required conditions is one involving disclosure of any Urea Formaldehyde Foam Insulation in the property and, as previously discussed, the purchaser should ensure that the words "to the best of the vendor's knowledge and belief" are not included in the disclosure.

A list of appliances and household effects which are to remain on the property at the time of the closing frequently appears as a condition to the agreement. For example, a purchaser may wish to have the appliances, window dressings and light fixtures at the property. The purchaser should not *assume* that such items will remain after closing and it is prudent to list all of the desired items on the agreement of purchase and sale. Strictly speaking, the law requires that a vendor leave with the property any fixtures actually attached to the property in a substantial manner. Nevertheless, vendors in the past have occasionally removed things like light fixtures, light switch covers and even doorbell covers, to the amazement of the purchaser on the day of closing. A condition stipulating that *all* fixtures, including light fixtures, are to remain in the property may help to avoid such a problem. The purchaser should realize, however, that a condition requiring appliances and light fixtures to remain does not mean that they will be in excellent working condition, or working condition at all. The purchaser should ensure that the appliances work prior to making his offer and, also, prior to completing his pre-closing inspection on the date of closing.

Finally, the purchaser should ensure that the vendor is required to provide a survey certificate, which disloses the boundaries of the property, the location of the house on the property and, if applicable, the location of the well, the septic system and the driveway on the property. Although the purchaser cannot *rely* on the vendor's survey certificate, it may be helpful to the purchaser's surveyor.

Another condition which should be stipulated in the agreement is that the purchaser has the right to complete a pre-closing inspection within 24 hours of the closing date. A pre-closing inspection allows the purchaser to review the property carefully before actually turning over his money to complete the transaction. The idea of the pre-closing inspection is to ensure that nothing substantial has changed on the property since the time that the agreement of purchase and sale was signed. For that reason, the purchaser should not complete the pre-closing inspection until the vendor has completely vacated the property. Once the vendor has vacated, it will be easy to observe any damage caused by the vendor in the course of the move (i.e., dents in walls, scratches on floors, broken windows, etc.). Sometimes, a vendor will move hastily and crack gyproc walls by banging them with furniture. Another not uncommon problem is caused when vendors drag heavy furniture or appliances across tile and hardwood floors, thereby causing deep scratches which are difficult or impossible to remove. On occasion, the pre-closing inspection will reveal more serious problems, such as basement flooding, broken pipes and broken windows. A pre-closing inspection in Summer or Fall may also reveal flea infestation from the vendor's pet.

If any problems are discovered in the course of the pre-closing inspection, the purchaser should notify his lawyer immediately. The purchaser's lawyer can then contact the vendor's lawyer, and arrangements will be made to rectify the problem. If the problem is not severe, the lawyers may agree to allow the purchaser to withhold from the purchase price a reasonable amount of money to repair the problem. In more serious cases, however, the closing may have to be postponed until the situation is resolved.

The purchaser should realize that a pre-closing inspection is not intended as a last-minute means of backing out of the agreement. If the purchaser has concerns about the quality or the condition of the property, he should include an inspection clause and have the property inspected soon after the signing of the agreement of purchase and sale. The pre-closing inspection clause is only for the purpose of discovering problems which did not exist in the property at the time the Agreement of purchase and sale was made.

The Cost of the Deal

Standard form agreements will likely indicate that the vendor is responsible for providing a deed to the purchaser on the closing date. The expense of providing such a deed should fall to the vendor, unless stipulated otherwise in the agreement itself. Normally, the vendor retains a lawyer who prepares the necessary deed and related documents (ie. UFFI warranty, tax certificate and statement of adjustments - for example). The vendor signs the documents, and the lawyer for the vendor must ensure that the funds he receives are properly paid pursuant to the calculations which appear on the statement of adjustments. In almost all cases, the purchase funds are paid by certified cheques from the trust account of the purchaser's lawyer. Prior to the closing time, therefore, the purchaser must ensure that his lawyer has received all of the purchase money, including any mortgage funds.

From the purchaser's perspective, it is important that all outstanding charges (or liens) against the property are paid and discharged before becoming the owner. If the vendor owes mortgage money to a bank, for example, if property taxes are owed or if a creditor has obtained a judgment against the vendor, all of those scenarios have probably resulted in charges against the vendor's bank. Instead of paying the whole purchase price to the vendor (and *hoping* that the vendor pays his debts), the purchaser should have his lawyer pay the vendor's debts *directly* from the purchase funds.

While the vendor usually incurs the cost of preparing the deed for the purchaser, the purchaser bears the cost of having a mortgage put in place for the benefit of his bank. A standard form agreement will formally stipulate the fact that the purchaser is solely responsible for this expense. Consequently, while the vendor's lawyer prepares a deed and related documents for signature by the vendor, the purchaser's lawyer (when the purchaser is borrowing money from the bank) will prepare the necessary documents for the purchaser's signature, provided that title to the property has passed his inspection. The vast majority of purchasers who borrow money from a bank sign mortgage documents in favour of that bank. Less often, purchasers are able to borrow money from their bank by means of a promissory note with a collateral mortgage. The point is that, whenever a purchaser borrows money from a bank to finance a property purchase, the bank will require some evidence of the loan, and will most often demand some form of security (a charge on the land) to protect its interest in the loan, as well. The lawyer for the purchaser will receive instructions from the bank and will prepare the necessary documentation on behalf of the purchaser.

While an agreement may stipulate that the vendor shall bear the cost of having a deed prepared and the purchaser shall bear the cost of having mortgage documents completed, the purchaser should recognize that the cost involved in *registering* the vendor's documents will be solely borne by him, unless stipulated otherwise in the agreement. When the closing of the transaction has occurred, the lawyer for the purchaser will have exchanged the purchase funds for the deeds and related closing documents. The lawyer's job is not complete, however, until he has taken the deed and the mortgage signed by the purchaser to the registry office in the county where the property is located. Once there, the lawyer for the purchaser must conduct a subsearch of the title to ensure that the vendor has not already sold the property to someone else; once it has been confirmed that the property to the title has remained satisfactory, the lawyer for the purchaser registers the deed, followed by the mortgage. The purchaser will be charged registration fees at the registry office and, in almost all cases, the purchaser will also be required to pay a land transfer tax to his Provincial Government. Neither the registration fees nor the land transfer tax are the responsibility of the vendor and, unless the agreement of purchase and sale states otherwise, the purchaser is required to pay these expenses.

Breaking Up Is Hard

An agreement should definitely indicate what is to happen if one of the parties cannot complete the transaction. Both the vendor and the purchaser should carefully read any such provision, however, and should ensure that they understand its ramifications.

Sometimes, an agreement will stipulate that, if the purchaser defaults in the transaction, the vendor will have two options:

1) keep any amount of deposit money paid by the purchaser to the vendor pursuant to the agreement of purchase and sale (which the purchaser agrees to be liquidated damages); or

2) the vendor may sue the purchaser to force the purchaser into completing the transaction.

A purchaser should be wary of the fact that standard form agreements have normally been prepared for the benefit of the vendor. While the forfeiture of deposit funds may not be particularly offensive to the purchaser if it is his fault that the transaction will not be completed, the notion that he may be forced to complete the transaction is not one to which he will probably agree. The purchaser would, therefore, prefer to limit his liability if he failed to complete the transaction, and he would be likely to perceive the forfeiture of his deposit as a fair penalty for doing so.

The vendor, on the other hand, wants to ensure that it is not easy for the purchaser to cancel the transaction. After all, the vendor does, upon signing an agreement, significantly jeopardize his ability to obtain a better deal from another purchaser and, if the first purchaser backs out of the agreement, the vendor will have to start again at square one in trying to sell his property. The vendor would want in the agreement a stipulation that a specific amount of money may be claimed by him from a purchaser as liquidated damages. A stipulation of that sort should bind the parties to an amount of damages to be incurred by the vendor if the transaction does not proceed at the fault of the purchaser. The vendor should realize that an agreement as to liquidated damages constitutes only half of his battle; the collection of these liquidated damages from the purchaser may be more difficult and, for that reason, the vendor should attempt to obtain the largest possible deposit from the purchaser. As previously discussed, a purchaser who has committed to a transaction by paying a significant deposit is less likely to abandon a transaction frivolously. A vendor will not want to limit his personal remedies to the mere collection of an agreed amount of liquidated damages. Obviously, the cancellation of a transaction by the purchaser usually constitutes an immense inconvenience to the vendor, and even the possibility of forcing the completion of a transaction by the purchaser is something that the vendor may wish to have available. The statement which often appears in the standard from agreements of purchase and sale, to the effect that the vendor may compel the purchaser to complete the transaction, is not objectionable from the vendor's perspective, despite the fact that it may not be particularly enforceable in a court room.

One issue which may not be addressed in a standard form agreement is the remedy available to the purchaser if the vendor fails to complete the transaction. Occasionally, a vendor who has decided to sell his property changes his mind after the agreement has been signed. If, for example, the vendor advertised his house for sale because he thought his employer was transferring him to another location, a change of plans by the employer may cause the vendor to back out of his agreement. In that event, the purchaser has been prejudiced, since he has most likely ended his search for a home and has made commitments to his bank and others in contemplation of his agreement to purchase the vendor's property. If the vendor refuses to complete the transaction, the purchaser may want more than simply the return of his deposit money. The purchaser should consider this issue before signing an agreement, and he may want to include a clause, if only handwritten, which stipulates an amount of liquidated damages which the vendor agrees to pay if the vendor fails to complete the transaction.

A standard form agreement of purchase and sale will normally stipulate that an offer, as contained in the agreement document, will be irrevocable by the purchaser until a particular time. The word irrevocable simply confirms that the purchaser cannot withdraw the offer before the time and date provided on the document. The vendor, consequently, is assured of a specific period of time in which he can review the offer and think about it, without having the offer withdrawn. Once the stipulated time period has lapsed, however, the purchaser can't withdraw the offer without notice to the vendor. As a result, the vendor is well advised to make his decision on the offer before the time listed on the document. Often, purchasers will attempt to put pressure on vendors by making the time for consideration of the offer very short. It is not unusual, for example, to see a purchaser make his offer irrevocable until midnight on the same date the offer is made; the vendor, being left with relatively little time to consider the offer, may feel pressured into accepting it. Purchasers should recognize that this tactic can easily backfire, as it may cause the vendor to become angry or frustrated with the purchaser. Beginning a potential relationship of this magnitude in a negative way can cause serious problems between the vendor and purchaser at a later date, so both parties should think twice before resorting to pressure tactics and hard bargaining.

A vendor who is faced with a short time in which to respond to an offer should be extremely careful not to act out of haste. Normally, vendors respond to offers of this sort by making relatively high counter-offers. Provided that a counter-offer is made within the stipulated time frame, the counter-offer has the effect of keeping the agreement document on the table for further consideration between the purchaser and the vendor. Sometimes, the price of the property is not the biggest issue to be negotiated; if that is the case, the vendor and the purchaser may both be required to make concessions in order to finalize an agreement.

If the purchaser does not have a legitimate motivation to have his offer accepted quickly, reasonable time should be afforded to the vendor to consider the offer and to respond appropriately. Again, it is critical to realize that the relationship between a vendor and purchaser can be very important, and it is prudent to start the relationship on a positive note whenever possible.

Conclusion

Once all of the terms of the agreement have been finalized, the parties should sign the document in the presence of a witness. The witness should not be one of the parties and, for that reason, it is normally a real estate agent who acts in this capacity. After the ink is on the paper, all of the parties are bound by the agreement and obligated to comply with its terms. Any doubts that the purchaser or vendor may have with regard to the agreement, or any changes which either of them may want to incorporate into it should be addressed BEFORE the agreement is signed, not after. Both parties should seriously consider having their lawyers review the document before signing it. You will want to know about any potential heartache before it happens, not afterwards.

THE HAPPY HOMEOWNER

Now you have reviewed *some* tips for improving your approach to four important aspects of house purchasing: selection of a great house buying team; how to choose a great place to live; finding great houses (and eliminating the not-so-great ones); and making a great agreement of purchase and sale. The previous chapters of this book do not address every issue, concern or potential problem that *should* cross your mind as you search for, and attempt to buy, your own great house; however, I hope that the information you have read is useful to you for the development of a concrete, step-by-step house-hunting plan. Additionally, I expect that the issues which *are* raised will cause you to think of even more important points for consideration.

Without any question, the extent of your happiness in the house you ultimately purchase will relate to your success in executing an effective home purchase plan. The more problems you are able to avoid, through careful examination and negotiation *before* buying, the fewer headaches you will experience *after* becoming a home owner. While it is likely impossible to completely eliminate risks in a large transaction such as a home purchase, it certainly is possible (and relatively easy) to reduce and minimize your risk exposure. Once you have done your homework properly, it will be time to enjoy the excitement and satisfaction of home *ownership*. Enter that phase of the process with confidence, knowing that you've take appropriate precautions. Furthermore, and in order to maximize the benefit of your careful work to this point, you should protect your investment of time, effort and money by following these simple steps.

- *Review your purchase documents once more before storing them.*

Make sure the purchase documents you receive from your lawyer and real estate agent confirm your understanding of the transaction. For most people, the week leading up to the house purchase is extremely hectic. Moving out of one home and into another; arranging for mailing address change forms, telephone installation, electric power accounts and other administrative issues; and making arrangements to move into your new home - these are all stressful and time-consuming processes. When the dust settles, your temptation will be to stuff the purchase documents in a drawer so that you can move on to more enjoyable pursuits (like painting, furniture arranging, etc.). Just before you put the documents out of your mind, though, take a few minutes to review them again, in order to ensure your understanding of issues such as outstanding property taxes, legal fees owed, property line locations and any special points or instructions that have been made to you by your home purchase team. Assuming the documents are consistent with your understanding of what has taken place, you will be able to close that chapter of the process with peace of mind.

- *Store your purchase documents in a safe place.*

You will be saving yourself future time and money if you keep your purchase documents in safe storage where you will be able to locate them on a moment's notice. If an issue should ever arise regarding your land, for example, you will want to have quick access to the documents which confirm your ownership. Additionally, if you should sell your house in the future, the documents will be particularly important for you to have available.

- *Perform regular maintenance on any well, septic system or similar property feature.*

Wells and septic systems do not always look after themselves. If your property is not connected to municipal services, you will likely save yourself a on future inconvenience if you conduct a recommended and scheduled maintenance on those systems. Many septic systems, for example, should be cleaned (pumped out) periodically; you will be able to obtain information in that regard from a suitable expert. As for a well, it is normally prudent to have the well water quality tested from time to time. Also check fixtures and related equipment; again, do this in accordance with advice from an expert.

On occasion, a well or septic system will malfunction which can be extraordinarily frustrating (not to mention costly). Save yourself from even the prospect of that grief by looking after those systems properly.

- *Do regular maintenance.*

You know that your house is not indestructible. Like most other man-made items, your house is susceptible to damage by weather, accidents and normal wear and tear. Look after your property by conducting periodic inspections and doing maintenance. Relatively straight forward efforts, such as painting, can save thousands of dollars in later repair costs if done when needed, not later.

Owning a home is one of the great aspirations of North Americans. Additionally, home ownership can be a wise investment, particularly if the home is located in a desirable area and is in good condition. Congratulations on making the effort to learn more about successful home purchase strategies; it is now up to you to implement your knowledge in a way that maximizes both the joy and the financial benefits to be gained from your new home!

APPENDIX

THREE-HOUSE INTERIOR
COMPARISON SHEET

	HOUSE 1		HOUSE 2		HOUSE 3	
	Yes	No	Yes	No	Yes	No
BASEMENT						
Unfinished	☐	☐	☐	☐	☐	☐
Concrete cracks	☐	☐	☐	☐	☐	☐
Sump pump	☐	☐	☐	☐	☐	☐
Evidence of past leakage	☐	☐	☐	☐	☐	☐
Old wiring	☐	☐	☐	☐	☐	☐
Renovations needed	☐	☐	☐	☐	☐	☐
Expert(s) concerned	☐	☐	☐	☐	☐	☐
KITCHEN						
Needs cupboards	☐	☐	☐	☐	☐	☐
Needs counter space	☐	☐	☐	☐	☐	☐
Insufficient dining area	☐	☐	☐	☐	☐	☐
Old appliances	☐	☐	☐	☐	☐	☐
Flooring damaged	☐	☐	☐	☐	☐	☐
Needs dishwasher	☐	☐	☐	☐	☐	☐
Expert(s) concerned	☐	☐	☐	☐	☐	☐

	HOUSE 1		HOUSE 2		HOUSE 3	
	Yes	No	Yes	No	Yes	No
BATHROOM						
Insufficient for needs	☐	☐	☐	☐	☐	☐
Fixtures damaged	☐	☐	☐	☐	☐	☐
Tiles require replacement	☐	☐	☐	☐	☐	☐
Expert(s) concerned	☐	☐	☐	☐	☐	☐
ALL OTHER ROOMS						
Ceilings damaged	☐	☐	☐	☐	☐	☐
Walls damaged	☐	☐	☐	☐	☐	☐
Insufficient closet space	☐	☐	☐	☐	☐	☐
Bedroom storage	☐	☐	☐	☐	☐	☐
Too small for furniture	☐	☐	☐	☐	☐	☐
Expert(s) concerned	☐	☐	☐	☐	☐	☐
ATTIC						
Evidence of intruders	☐	☐	☐	☐	☐	☐
Evidence of leakage	☐	☐	☐	☐	☐	☐
Insufficient insulation	☐	☐	☐	☐	☐	☐
Expert(s) concerned	☐	☐	☐	☐	☐	☐
TOTAL	☐	☐	☐	☐	☐	☐

ABOUT THE AUTHOR

Kelly VanBuskirk is a lawyer who has represented a great number of house buyers, sellers, owners, real estate agents, contractors and municipalities in real estate disputes. He has a Master's degree in Law, and has been an invited guest lecturer to countless organizations. The WebSite address of Kelly's law firm is: www.lawsoncreamer.com